EXORCISM

BY OLGA HOYT
EXORCISM

Franklin Watts
New York | London | 1978

Photographs courtesy of:

The New York Public Library Picture Collection:
pp. 7, 13, 20, 50;

United Press International:
pp. 77, 88, 89, 90, 94, 96, 99, 108;

The Honolulu Advertiser:
p. 106.

Library of Congress Cataloging in Publication Data

Hoyt, Olga.
  Exorcism.

  Bibliography: p.
  Includes index.
  SUMMARY: Discusses the practice of exorcism with descriptions of possessed people from ancient times to the present.
  1. Exorcism—History—Juvenile literature. [1. Exorcism—History] I. Title.
BF1559.H68   133.4'27   77-17084
ISBN 0-531-01480-0

Copyright © 1978 by Olga Hoyt
All rights reserved
Printed in the United States of America
6 5 4 3 2

CONTENTS

Introduction | 3

The Ancients | 5

Christ, Early Christians, and the Middle Ages | 16

Fifteenth and Sixteenth Centuries | 24

Seventeenth and Eighteenth Centuries | 33

The Nineteenth Century | 45

The Twentieth Century | 67

Notes | 111

Bibliography | 116

Index | 118

EXORCISM

INTRODUCTION

Over a decade ago began a phenomenon which could be called the "occult explosion." For some as yet undefined reason people all over the world began to turn to mysticism, in one form or another. Satanic cults sprang up throughout Europe. Ten thousand German citizens openly dabbled in witchcraft; three times that number joined witch covens in England. In the United States a Gallup poll showed that 60 percent of the population believed in the devil.[1] Interest rose in Ouija boards, I Ching, astrology and horoscopes, and alternative churches. No definitive answer has been given as to why this seemingly sudden trend began or why its growth has continued to the present.

In this climate of mysticism the devil began to get his due—far more than he had had for hundreds of years. The Bishop of Exeter in England acknowledged the presence and power of "evil forces" and set up a commission in 1963 to examine guidelines for exorcism by the clergy, since requests for driving out the devil were rising alarmingly.[2] Pope Paul VI, head of the Roman Catholic Church, in 1972 devoted a sermon to the very real existence of Satan.[3] But perhaps the devil received the greatest public attention when *The Exorcist* was shown all over the world in 1974.[4]

Here was a bizarre film, based (with dramatic and ghoulish additions) on an actual exorcism performed some years previously over a young boy. The film caused an uproar. Movie-goers were shocked and frightened; some fainted, some became nauseated. Yet millions of people paid $121 million to see the film.[5] Some clergy protested that the work should be condemned for showing how believable human possession by the devil can be; others claimed the film was sheer pornography.[6] No matter the criticism against the film, it brought the subject of demonic possession and, of course, the resultant exorcism of the devil, to the forefront of Western public consciousness, as had not been done for centuries.

The uncertainties of our times have helped bring about this intensified interest in the occult, and it seems likely this trend will grow. From Hollywood comes the report that almost every movie company currently has five or six devil movies in the works. They earn millions for the makers, and, according to one film executive, satisfy the public interest in "mysticism, the supernatural, and the psychic. It's a kind of pop religion." [7]

Yet the belief in devils and exorcism has existed since the early days of ancient civilizations, long before Christ. It might be instructive to see how people throughout the centuries have believed in the devil and exorcism—and how they still do today.

OLGA HOYT

THE ANCIENTS

One May night in 1966, Bernadette Hasler, a pretty blond seventeen-year-old, was attacked with walking sticks, a riding crop, plastic tubes, and birch rods in a Swiss mountain chalet. Six adults of a fanatic religious cult alternately prayed and beat the young girl as they tried to exorcise the devil from her body.

Numb and submissive after several hours, Bernadette was ordered to crawl on all fours outside to wash her bloodstained clothing.

Then her torturers demanded to know: Did she repent her sin of *Teufelsbuhlschaft*, coupling-with-the-devil? The young girl murmured "yes" and was sent to bed.

The next morning she was dead.

It was, as reported by the Swiss newspaper *Blick*, "an orgy of brutality . . . in order to drive out the devil . . . and make her feel the righteous wrath of the Lord." [1]

Here was a shocking, terrifying exorcism, a murder in the name of religion. Asked if such savagery was necessary, one of the participants answered: "How else do you drive the devils out? As God is my witness, I bear no guilt for Bernadette's death." [2]

That such a brutal exorcism could have taken place in a sophisticated European culture in the twentieth century is almost beyond belief. It might have been more understandable if it had happened three thousand years ago, for the practice of exorcism is that old.

Long before Christianity, in the ancient civilizations of Babylonia and Assyria, the devil and demons were thought of as commonplace.

There were hundreds of these creatures—demons, devils, djinn, ghouls, ghosts, vampires, evil spirits—and they were everywhere. They lived in the deserts, in the mountains, in caves, in the marshlands, in graves. They rode with the wind into the cities; they slipped into houses. These early people knew that these creatures all about them caused disaster and disease. They were literally an army of evil that had to be warded off, and if they possessed a person or a place they had to be driven out.

In these ancient times the one who drove out the demons, the exorcist, was a very important person. He was in constant demand to rid the sick of the demons which had caused disease. His incantations kept temples sacred. At burials his presence was required to be sure a demon did not linger to plague the living.

The Babylonian exorcist did not claim that he himself had power over the devil; he sent his prayers to gods such as Ea and Marduk who drove the devil away. The center of Babylonian worship was at a place called Eridu. Here the ancient exorcism rites were celebrated constantly in a pattern that was to pass down through the centuries.

The exorcist first called the demon by name, speaking to the gods and to the demon directly, pleading with it to

A Babylonian god destroying a one-eyed demon of fire

leave the possessed. Since there were many demons, the exorcist recited scores of names, to be sure that the particular demon involved was addressed.

When a priest performed an exorcism, the patient would be on a bed on which were tied black and white objects. The priest made his appeal to Marduk, the God Ea's son. As he chanted, "By heaven be ye exorcised. By Earth be ye exorcised," he sprinkled water around the patient. Then he sprinkled perfume about the room of the possessed. When he was finished, he pronounced the demon gone—exorcised. At other times the exorcist placed flour around the patient. Often he brought animals into the room, so that the demon would go into the beasts.

One exorcist's technique to drive the evil out of a person was to force it into seven loaves of bread, seven because the number had a magical significance. These were then taken out to the desert, where it did not matter if the evil spirit escaped.[3]

Many of the ancient chants and prayers used to cast out the devil were preserved on clay tablets. One, written about 3000 B.C. (and now in a London museum), was found in the temple of a Babylonian ruler, Assurbanipal, at Nineveh. It was a prayer to the gods Ea, Shamash, and Marduk from a man suffering from "a tyrannical ghost" that possessed his "body and soul." The man was pleading to the gods to rid him of the creature. He said the "horrible specter . . . fastened itself on my back and will not let go of me. . . . He strikes terror into me, sends forth poison and he makes the hair on my head stand up. He taketh the power from my body, he maketh mine eyes stand out, he plagueth my back, he poisoneth my flesh, he plagueth my whole body."[4]

The ancients believed that most sicknesses were caused by evil spirits. In Egypt sickness itself was considered to be a demon. If a person was ill, it was because he was possessed by a demon. No one was immune to these demonic attacks, but since most people recovered from flu and stomachaches and other common ailments, the Egyptian exorcists were considered unusually adept in curing these demon-induced diseases.

Here is an old Egyptian exorcism for use against sickness in children:

> Go hence, thou who comest in darkness, whose nose is turned backwards, whose face is upside down and who knowest not why thou hast come. . . . I will not let thee do him harm. Hast thou come to take him with thee? I will not let thee carry him away. . . .[5]

Perhaps the most famous of the ancient Egyptian exorcisms is on a stone marker in the temple of the God Khonsu at Thebes. The inscription was written in the fourth century B.C., but it is thought that it refers to a much earlier legend.[6] The story was recorded in the temple to impress all with the wonders and powers of the great God Khonsu in driving out an evil spirit.

One day the king of Egypt, Rameses II, was visiting in Mesopotamia and all the princes of the land came to pay tribute to him, bringing many kinds of gifts—gold, silver, lapis lazuli, copper, and rare woods. Each in his turn presented the king with an offering. When the prince of Bekhten approached the king he led forth his eldest daughter, a beautiful young woman. The king fell in love with her, and took her back to Egypt, where he married her, and gave her the name of Neferou Ra, the beauty of the sun. Time passed happily. Then, some years later, an ambassador from the land of Bekhten suddenly arrived, asking for help. The young sister of Queen Neferou Ra, Bint-Reschid, was possessed by an evil disease. Many had tried to cure her but they had failed. The prince begged the king to send one of his wise men to her. The king consulted his magic books and his learned men, and selected Tehutiem-heb to go to Bekhten with the prince's emissary.

But when Tehutiem-heb saw the languishing Bint-Reschid, he realized that he was unable to help her, for she was possessed by an evil spirit. His power was not great enough to drive this malevolent force out of the young girl. In distress, the prince sent another messenger to King Rameses, to ask if perhaps this time a god could be sent to cure the queen's sister. It so happened that at the moment the agent arrived, the king was worshipping in the temple at Thebes, and he thought to send the statue of the God Khonsu. To be sure that the statue had enough power to cure, the god himself gave it a fourfold measure of magical power.

Thus a procession set out for Bekhten: the statue, along with other figures of lesser gods, with horsemen riding alongside to protect the caravan. They arrived after a year and five months, and when they came into the presence of the prince's daughter the evil spirit immediately departed peacefully, and there was joy throughout the land.[7]

In ancient Egypt the exorcism was performed by a combination of a physician—to cure the ailment—and a priest—to drive out the demon of disease. Sometimes the two functions were combined in one learned person, a doctor-priest.

The general practice was to use chants along with certain rituals, such as this one preserved on an Egyptian papyrus, which was used in the case of snake bites:

First the exorcist brought to the victim a painted hawk made of wood, which had two feathers on its head. He began his prayer over the hawk. This prayer was an appeal to the demon who was addressed by first calling on the God Horus. As the exorcist chanted over the hawk, he opened the bird's mouth and gave it bread, beer, and incense. He intoned:

> Horus conjures thee, he cuts thee off, he spits thee out, and thou risest not up but fallest down. . . . Thou are turned back . . . thou creepest away. . . . Horus has slain it by his magic. Stand up, thou who wast prostrate. Horus has restored thee to life. . . . Turn back, thou snake, conjured is thy poison. . . . Behold the magic of Horus is powerful against thee. Flow out, thou poison, come forth upon the ground.

After the ritual over the wooden bird, the exorcist placed the hawk on the face of the patient, and recited the spell again.[8]

This traditional ritual for snake bite was acclaimed as a great success since so many patients survived.

Ancient Persia, too, had its rituals for exorcism. One of the best known of the early religious leaders there was Zoroaster, who lived in the sixth century B.C. He is known best as the founder of the religion Zoroastrianism, which holds that the forces of good and evil constantly war over the soul of man. He also was considered by many to be the first magician, and much of the material in books of magic ritual has been attributed to him.

Zoroaster had still a third claim to fame: He was an exorcist. Like the Babylonians and Egyptians he employed a combination of prayer and ritual to drive out the evil spirits. As he spoke the prescribed chants, Zoroaster sprinkled the possessed person with water. After a few drops the evil spirit went down from the head to the shoulder. More water drove the spirit to the chest; then, on down to the bottom of the foot, then to the toe. Since there was no other place on the body to go, the evil spirit might fly away from the victim's toe, buzzing angrily as it went.[9]

Demonic possession was common also in ancient India, where the people believed in innumerable demons and gods of madness who seized upon humans. If one broke a religious law, or stayed alone in an empty house, or visited a burial place at night, one was vulnerable to seizure by a demon.

There were many different sorts of evil spirits. The way a possessed person behaved would denote which demon was present.

> ... the man possessed by a *daitya* is spiteful, hot-tempered, proud; he called himself a god, likes spirituous liquors and meat. He who is possessed by a *gandharva* sings and dances, bedecks, bathes, and anoints himself. He who is possessed by a demon snake has red eyes, a fixed stare, his walk is tortuous and unsteady, he puts out his tongue, licks the corners of his lips, likes milk, honey and sweet things. He who is possessed by a *yaksa* is voluptuous, lascivious, prodigal, talkative, and staggers like a drunkard in his walk. He who is possessed by a *pisaka* is uneasy,

**Zoroaster,
a Persian exorcist
who lived in the
sixth century B.C.**

gluttonous and dirty; he has no memory, runs hither and thither, tears his flesh with his nails and walks naked.[10]

A great exorcist of ancient India was the mother of Buddha. When she was pregnant with Buddha, the legend goes, she had amazing powers of curing those possessed by demons, especially young girls and women. These females "running about naked and covered with dust, regained their senses by the sight of Maya and being endowed with memory, understanding, and correct notions, returned to their homes." [11]

An ancient Jewish exorcism used by a celebrated magician involved long chants, recited after a weird mixture of the juice of green fruits and lotus pith, which had been heated with marjoram, was poured over the patient.[12]

King Solomon, an important biblical figure, was perhaps the most noted of the Jewish magicians and exorcists.

Solomon was king of Israel in the tenth century B.C. He gained a great reputation because of his wisdom and his power over all devils. It was said that an angel of God had given him a magic seal ring made of brass and iron. With it he could control the devils. Solomon's fame was so great that in the early Christian era his methods and formulas concerning the devil were included in a magical textbook (called a *grimoire*) entitled *Testament of Solomon*.[13]

Flavius Josephus, a Jewish historian, wrote in the first century A.D. about Solomon and his charms, which were still being used in Israel to drive away demons. Flavius told of seeing a man named Eleazar perform exorcisms before the Roman Emperor Vespasian and his soldiers, curing "people possessed by demons."

Eleazar placed under the seal of a magic ring one of the magic roots mentioned by Solomon. Then he held the ring under the nostrils of the possessed person, reciting the charms Solomon had used. As the person smelled the ring, the demon was drawn out and the person was cured. Eleazar, in the name of Solomon, then ordered the demon never to return into the man.

According to Flavius, all the spectators were especially awed by the movement of a cup of water that had been placed a short distance from the man. Eleazar ordered the demon to tip over the cup as he left the man, and the demon did so.[14]

CHRIST, EARLY CHRISTIANS, AND THE MIDDLE AGES

Many Christians do not know it but Jesus Christ was an exorcist. Matthew, Mark, and Luke tell many tales in their gospels in the New Testament to attest to Jesus' ability as exorcist and healer. Mark told the story of a dumb man possessed of a devil who was brought to Jesus. Jesus then cast out the devil and the dumb man spoke.[1] Mark also speaks of Jesus casting out many other devils. Jesus ". . . suffered not the devils to speak because they knew him." "Evil spirits," "unclean spirits," devils, and "demons" all were exorcised by Jesus.[2]

Perhaps the most spectacular incident was that which concerned the Gadarene demon. Mark, Matthew, and Luke all tell that story:

One day Jesus and some of his disciples were crossing the Lake of Genesareth from Galilee, when a storm arose. The disciples were alarmed, but Jesus spoke to the wind and the water: "Hush! Be still," and the lake became flat and calm. When they landed safely in the land of the Gadarenes, they came upon a naked wild man, who lived in the tombs. He had been running about in the mountains, crying and cutting himself on the stones. When he saw Jesus, he ran up to him, asking for help. Jesus asked his name and he replied: "My name is Legion, for we are many." Jesus then addressed the demon in the possessed man: "Go out of the man thou unclean spirit." And the spirits themselves spoke to Jesus and suggested that he send them into a great herd of swine grazing nearby. Jesus gave them permission to go into the pigs. They left the man, entered the swine, and suddenly the whole herd jumped into the sea, taking the evil with them. And Jesus told the man to go to his home and tell his friends "how great things the Lord hath done for thee. . . ." [3]

The story of this miraculous cure spread far and wide and people came from all over to see the madman, now peaceful and happy.

Throughout Israel self-proclaimed exorcists who journeyed from town to town began to include the name of Jesus in their rites. The word of his power over evil drew many followers to him. Many of those who had worked magic threw away their tricks in awe, because they recognized Christ's power over evil.

The early Christian leaders continued to believe in possession by evil. Zealously they set about ridding the whole world of the demons that seemed to be everywhere. Harnack, a historian, wrote that by the second century A.D., "the whole world and the atmosphere surrounding it was peopled with devils. . . . They sat upon thrones and surrounded the infant's cradle. The earth . . . became in very truth a hell." [4]

By this time the church had developed its own rituals of exorcism. Some of the usual procedures were followed: recitation, prayers, and exorcism. Added to these were the signs of the cross, followed by fast and prayer. The ritual was so simple that it could be done by the most unsophisticated persons. Of course, it was necessary that the victim have a firm belief in God in order to be cured.

The early Christian Gregory the Great told a story of a poor girl possessed by devils. Her parents took her to a local witch, hoping she could drive out the demons. The witch took the girl to a river and washed her and chanted over her. Finally the witch drove out one devil. But that one devil was replaced by a horde of devils who swarmed into the shrieking and thrashing girl's body. The parents were dismayed, and shamefacedly carried her to the bishop, confessing their wrong-doing to him. They acknowledged that they should never have sought the black magic of the witch. The parents pleaded with the bishop, who finally agreed to exorcise the child. He had a most difficult time for he was fighting scores of demons, but finally, after many days, the bishop's prayers drove the devils out of the girl, and she was cured.[5]

The early Christians were eager to perform exorcisms, for by their successes they hoped to gather converts to the new religion. Many people did flock to the church for this reason because the belief in devils and demons was almost universal and the clergy promised the people freedom from the diabolical creatures.

In the fifth century A.D., Saint Benedict was greatly revered because he had defeated the evil spirits who had plagued the building of his new monastery atop Monte Cassino. Everyone knew the place was full of devils, for at one time witches held their satanic rites in this place. Saint Benedict was constantly called upon to exorcise monks who were possessed by the evil spirits still lurking in the area. He was so successful in his exorcisms that a medal created with his cross on it was used as a protection against the evil.

The belief in demonic possession and exorcism was not confined to Italy. In France in the sixth century Gregory of Tours told how on feast days possessed people would enter the churches in a wild state and dash about breaking lamps and disturbing the services. But the moment a drop of oil from the lamps of the holy place fell on them—as it was sure to do—the demons departed and they were freed.[6]

Through the centuries the belief in possession and cure continued, and with the growth of Christianity the word of the skill and power of the churchmen-exorcists spread across Europe. Biographies and legends of the saints up into the Middle Ages contain hundreds of cases of exorcisms performed by Christian churchmen through prayer to God.

Saint Bernard of Clairvaux was one of the more highly acclaimed exorcists. Generally his exorcisms were made before crowds of people in the churches. Stories of his successes were spread by word of mouth. Soon many men and women sought his help. Young children in particular were brought to him to be cured.

One day in Milan an old woman was swept up to the church in a crowd hurrying to mass. She had been a respectable matron, but now she was a frightful sight because the devil had entered into her some years before. She could not speak, she stuck out her tongue and she ground her teeth. When Saint Bernard saw her horrible appearance, he knew that the devil was in her. As he began his mass, he asked the crowd to pray for the unhappy woman, who was brought close to the altar. Saint Bernard cautioned her to stay where she was, but she began to move

A fifteenth century
depiction of
Saint Bernard of Clairvaux

about and the devil within her drove her to lash out at the saint with a good strong kick. The churchman appealed for God's help to cure this unfortunate woman, and he recited the Lord's Prayer. Then he spoke to the devil in the woman: "I command thee, evil spirit, to come out of His servant and dare to touch her no more thereafter." The saint then turned back to the altar and continued his regular church rites. When the benediction was given to the people, suddenly the woman was cured. The devil was gone, and she was normal. She gave her thanks, and the congregation arose in jubilation and cried out honors to God and the church bells rang.[7]

It was small wonder, then, that Saint Bernard, performing such miracles through prayer, was known throughout many lands. Wherever he went he was sought out to aid those possessed by unclean spirits. His biographer, Ernaldus, wrote of the saint's conversations with a particularly saucy demon. This demon spoke through the mouth of a possessed woman who had been brought to the saint. A crowd had gathered to witness the battle between the saint and the devil. Immediately the devil spoke up, taunting the saint.

"No," said the devil, "this eater of leeks, this devourer of cabbages shall not drive me away." The saint ignored the insults, for he knew the devil was trying to anger and confuse him. He began to pray to God to save the woman. The devil continued to speak, but now was contrite, saying that it really did not wish to stay within the woman, that once it had seen Jesus Christ, but had then fallen away with Lucifer. All assembled heard the devil speak through the voice of the woman. Saint Bernard continued to pray and at last the devil departed and the woman was herself again. She thanked the saint and went home. But when she reached the doorstep of her house the devil returned. The woman's husband sought out the saint again, who this time spent the whole night in prayer, driving the devil out once more. But fearing his return, the saint ordered a sign to be made which read: "In the name of our Lord Jesus Christ I command thee, demon, to dare to touch this woman no more." He fastened the sign around the woman's neck, and the devil never came to her again.[8]

In the twelfth century Saint Norbert of Magdeburg was also noted for his exorcisms. And he, too, had conversations with the devil through the mouths of the possessed.

One day a woman who was suffering from the evil within her was brought to him, and soon the words began to fly. The devil spoke: "For thee nor for any other will I come forth today. . . ." And the exorcism proved difficult for the saint. After praying all day without success, in the evening he ordered the woman plunged into holy water. It was done. Her hair was also cut, for Saint Norbert was afraid that the devil might be able to hold onto her by her hair. But by darkness the devil was still in the woman, and reluctantly the saint sent her home. For the next twenty-four hours the saint fasted and prayed for the woman, who was again brought to the mass. Saint Norbert prayed and performed the rituals of the mass, and finally the demon cried out through the mouth of the woman: "I burn! I burn! I am dying! I am dying! I will go forth." And it did. The girl fell to the floor. She was then taken back to her home where she recovered completely. The devil never returned.[9]

Throughout the next century cases of possession were reported throughout Europe. Some were most odd. Diagnosticians of later generations might consider these "possessions" caused by physical or mental conditions, but the people at the time believed that the evil spirits were responsible. One of these strange occurrences was a dancing mania. Groups of people suddenly began acting in a hysterical fashion, running about, jumping convulsively, leaping and dancing. One such mania occurred in 1318 at Strasbourg, France, and the participants were taken to the chapel of Saint Vitus for exorcism. The possessed people and the priests all believed that evil spirits had taken over the dancing bodies. Thus the term "Saint Vitus dance" has come down through the generations meaning a convulsive physical condition.[10]

Similar cases were reported in Aachen, Germany, in 1374, and later in Belgium and Holland.[11]

By this time much erratic behavior was classed as possession, and the only cure was thought to be exorcism.

FIFTEENTH AND SIXTEENTH CENTURIES

The practice of exorcism was by no means confined to the Christian religion. In the fifteenth century Leo Africanus traveled widely in northern Africa, where the Moslem religion dominated. He reported that the exorcists there also talked to the evil spirit in the possessed. The exorcist called the spirit and asked its name. He inquired how the spirit got into the body, and through which part of the body. After he learned these facts, the exorcist called on the devil to come out. Sometimes the exorcists were successful, sometimes they were not. But because they did on occasion drive out devils, the people thought they had great power. The exorcists often excused their failures by claiming that the spirit was disobedient, or that it really was not an evil spirit but one that was heavenly.[1]

Still, the majority of exorcisms performed at this time were in Christian societies. As Christianity spread, the use of exorcism increased. It generally was performed before baptism into the Church, for if a person had been a pagan before becoming a convert to Christianity, the person had been vulnerable to demons and evil spirits.

FIFTEENTH AND SIXTEENTH CENTURIES | 25

In 1566 a case of mass possession occurred in Amsterdam. Thirty children began to show the same symptoms: they foamed at the mouth, they had convulsions, they fell to the ground. Protestant clergy were called, but they could not drive out the evil forces. The parents of the children then went to magicians, but the children got worse, vomiting "pins and needles." In the hysteria of the times, their plight was attributed to witchcraft. Eventually they recovered when the witches who had reportedly bewitched the children were discovered.[2]

In Vienna in 1583, when a sixteen-year-old girl was found to be possessed, the Jesuits spent eight weeks exorcising her, to drive out the evil that was causing her severe cramps.

At the end of the exorcism the priests claimed they had driven out 12,652 living demons from her. As so often was the case in those times, the girl's grandmother was accused of witchcraft. The monks said she kept those demons masked as flies in a jar. The grandmother was turned over to the authorities and tortured as a witch. She confessed to witchcraft and was burned to death.[3]

Missionaries to Japan brought back a number of stories of possession. One of these occurred in 1565 in Bungo, where a family had been possessed by a demon for a hundred years. The same demon stayed with the family one generation after another. The father had tried to rid them of it by appeasing the gods, but the devil continued to plague the family. The son was possessed and could not eat or drink for fifteen days. In despair, the father called a Christian priest to come to the house. The priest instructed the young boy to pronounce the Trinity. The boy did as he was told, and the devil left him. The daughter wanted to be converted to the Catholic faith, but found that the devil made it almost impossible. She could not make the sign of the cross without trembling and falling into convulsions. It was only after long hours of prayer by many Christian friends of the family that the demon reluctantly left her and the rest of the family.[4]

In these years the practice of exorcism was a "practical" necessity in societies where demons, devils, and evil spirits were everywhere. So, many of the clergy practiced exorcism as a regular part of their religious duties, and exorcism usually brought them honor and esteem. However, this was not always the case. At one time in sixteenth-century England exorcists were actually persecuted.

William Weston was a Jesuit missionary priest who had been educated at Oxford and in Paris. He joined the missionary society in 1575 and taught and worked in Spain until he was called home to England in 1584. He had performed many exorcisms in Spain. But when he returned to England he found that these practices were detested by the authorities. Indeed, as a Roman Catholic, Father Weston was suspect from the first. England had broken away from Rome in 1527. Queen Elizabeth was on the throne and she, a Protestant, would soon go to war with Catholic Spain. Thus, Weston, returned from Spain, fell under suspicion immediately as a possible agent of Rome and the Spanish monarchy.

Two noblemen, ardent Catholics, asked Weston to perform exorcisms in their homes for a number of distressed persons. Weston agreed, but he cautioned that the rites should be performed in the greatest secrecy. Weston and several other priests did perform a number of exorcisms, but after some months someone talked about them, and greatly exaggerated accounts of these rites began to circulate. Finally the reports reached the Privy Council. This body not only expressed disapproval of the exorcisms, but ordered a number of the exorcists seized and killed. Others were sent to jail, William Weston among them. Weston remained in jail from 1586 to 1599, when he was taken to the infamous prison, the Tower. He was banished from the country in 1603, went to Spain and worked as a college rector. He died there in 1615.[5]

Weston's plight was a reflection of the religious wars that spread across Europe in his time. Roman Catholic exorcists were feared and hated by the Protestants, and were often regarded as witches. But in Catholic countries exorcism continued to thrive.

In 1583 the French National Synod of Rheims, noting the rise of the number of exorcisms performed and also the number of cases of false possession, issued a report cautioning priests who would be exorcists:

> Before the priest undertakes an exorcism, he ought diligently to inquire into the life of the possessed, into his condition, reputation, health, and other circumstances; and he should consult with wise, prudent, and well-informed persons, rather than those who might be too credulous and inclined to be deceived. Melancholics, lunatics, and persons bewitched often declare themselves to be possessed by the devil; those people, however, are more in need of a doctor than of an exorcist.[6]

(In modern times physicians would diagnose many

cases of "possession" as epilepsy. The victims of this disease appeared to grin and laugh wildly—muscle spasms of mouth and face—and to dance wildly—again, muscle spasms of arms and legs. Our superstitious ancestors considered these signs of evil, however, not of illness.)

It was indeed difficult for the churchmen to identify what they believed to be true cases of diabolical possession. Witchcraft was flourishing in Europe, black magic was at its peak. Accusations of witchcraft were everyday occurrences, and many innocent people were persecuted and hanged or burned for their alleged crimes. Within this atmosphere of fear and superstition many cases of "possession" turned out to be frauds, and some exorcists to be impostors.

One exorcist of note was John Darrel, a young Protestant minister in Nottingham, England. In 1586, when he was still in his twenties, he first tried his hand at exorcism in his own village. A seventeen-year-old girl, Katherine Wright, seemed to be possessed by a devil. After visiting her Darrel declared that she was truly possessed by an evil spirit, which he would exorcise. Darrel prayed over the girl for eight hours, but she seemed no better. Unwilling to admit failure as an exorcist, Darrel declared that Katherine had been bewitched by a woman named Margaret Roper, with whom she had recently quarreled. Margaret Roper, said Darrel, had sent a demon into Katherine. Katherine agreed that this must be true, and the authorities arrested Margaret Roper for witchcraft. The justice of the peace, however, found the accusation invalid, and severely rebuked Darrel for his part in the matter. Darrel narrowly escaped arrest.

This unsuccessful foray into exorcism was soon forgotten. Darrel went about his ministerial tasks. Ten years passed before he came to public attention again. This time he became involved in the possession case of a young boy in Burton-upon-Trent, Derby.

Thomas Darling had "fits," in which he saw green angels and a green cat. His behavior became increasingly erratic, and a doctor was called in. The diagnosis: The boy must have been bewitched. This seemed likely, since Thomas's condition grew worse. He went into convulsions when the Bible was read aloud to him. He started talking about a "little old woman" who wore a "broad-brimmed hat." Two women in the neighborhood whom the authorities had long suspected of being witches were brought to the magistrates for examination, and after questioning, one of them was put in jail. She was tortured, and confessed to being a witch. She died in jail before she could be executed.

Unfortunately Thomas Darling still did not improve, and John Darrel tried his hand at exorcising the demon. Actually, Darrel, an accomplished ventriloquist, managed to produce rough voices that appeared to come from Thomas, which he said was the devil speaking. Darrel prayed over the boy, and shortly thereafter pronounced him "cured." Indeed, Thomas was well again.

This case raised John Darrel's reputation as an exorcist, and it was not long afterward that he was called in to the case of the Starchie children in Lancashire. Ann Starchie was nine, and she twitched a lot. John was ten, and he was "compelled to shout" on his way to school. Then suddenly their conditions became much worse: they had fits, vomited blood, and shouted and barked. Their father knew something had to be done, so he consulted Edmund Hartley, a famous magician, and Hartley gave the children various charms. But Starchie and the magician had a falling out about the money to be paid. Starchie then claimed that Hartley was the cause of all their troubles. He cited one instance in which a visitor and a servant in the household joined the children in their howling and noise-making. Was that not proof of bewitchment?

Hartley, who had been in trouble before on similar charges, was arrested and brought before a justice of the peace. He was accused of constantly kissing the Starchie children while trying to "cure" them. That was how, said the authorities, he had put evil spirits into them. He was also accused of drawing magic circles on the ground.

He denied it all. Nevertheless he was convicted and hanged.

Then John Darrel entered the picture. He and his assistant, George More, performed an exorcism. After several days of prayers, they "drove out the devils," and the children were pronounced cured.

The Starchie case made John Darrel a national figure. In 1597 he was called to cure a young musician of Nottingham, William Somers. Somers had known Darrel and followed his career. Now William was possessed: He used strange gestures and at times he broke into laughter and began to dance. Darrel came to exorcise the evil spirits, for he believed the boy to be possessed as he showed all the classic symptoms. People around Somers were also convinced that it was possession, for each time Darrel mentioned a symptom, the boy exhibited it. He "tore; he foamed; he wallowed; his face was drawn awry; his eyes would stare and his tongue hang out. . . ."[7] Darrel stood over the boy and delivered sermons, and read prayer after prayer. At last Somers lay still on the ground; it was as though he were dead. Then, after fifteen minutes, he stood up, said that he was cured and the demon gone.

Darrel left with a reputation even greater than it had been. However, Somers did not remain cured. This time Somers accused thirteen women of being witches and causing his illness. Darrel agreed with this judgment, but the authorities did not. So although the women had been arrested, all but two were released. All this accusation and investigation caused quite a stir in the community, and aroused some of the town's more skeptical citizens. They managed to persuade the judges to order Somers taken to the house of correction, and there under pressure he admitted that Darrel had coached him in the antics of possession. It had been a great hoax.

When that news came out, it caused so great a scandal that the matter came to the attention of church authorities. A church commission examined Somers, who now reversed his position, and said that he had been coerced into telling lies about Darrel. Then Somers fell into another fit, and thrashed about so much the members of the commission felt that he was now telling the truth and that he was indeed possessed. The Lord Chief Justice decided to get to the bottom of the puzzling case. He had Somers brought to court, where once again Somers said that he had been prompted by Darrel into feigning possession. The Lord Chief Justice was so angered by the fraud that he called it to the attention of the Bishop of London. The Bishop professed himself shocked by the perfidy of the whole matter, and he called a church council. In the end, Darrel and his assistant, More, were deposed from the ministry and sent to prison.

This case drew much public attention. So many pamphlets and books were written about it, and so famous did it become in England that the scandal even found its way into contemporary plays. One playwright wrote these lines for an actor:

> It is the easiest thing, Sir, to be done.
> As plaine as fizzling: roule but wi' your eyes,
> And foame at th' mouth. A little castle-soape
> Will do't, to rub your lips: And then a nutshell,
> With toe and touchwood in it to spit fire,
> Did you ner'e read, Sir, little *Darrel's* tricks,
> With the boy *o'Burton* and the 7 in *Lancashire*
> Sommers at *Nottingham*? All these do teach it.
> And wee'l give out, Sir, that your wife ha's bewitch'd you.
> (Jonson in *The Devell is an Asse*)[8]

Not long after this—in 1604—a convocation revised the English church canons. Rule 72 clarified the position of the church on exorcism:

> No minister or ministers shall . . . without the license or direction of the Bishop . . . attempt upon any pretence whatsoever either of possession or obsession, by fasting or prayer, to cast out any devil or devils, under pain of the imputation of imposture or cozenage, and deposition from the ministry.[9]

SEVENTEENTH AND EIGHTEENTH CENTURIES

During the witch craze in Europe so many varieties of exorcism were brought into play that the official Church rites covering exorcism became confused and contradictory. To remedy this, early in the seventeenth century (1614) the Vatican formulated the *Rituale Romanum*. And though this was revised in 1952, it still stands as the basic document covering exorcism within the Roman Catholic Church.

The rite for the ordination of exorcists was spelled out in complete detail: the motions, the specific prayers, and cautions. Bishops were directed to say:

> Ye must duly know what ye are about to undertake. For an exorcist must cast out devils . . . and by . . . the words of exorcism unclean spirits are driven out from the bodies of those who are obsessed. Be careful therefore that as ye drive out devils from the bodies of others, so ye banish all uncleanness and evil from your own bodies lest ye fall beneath the power of those spirits. . . .

The bishop then warns that "the enemy may claim a share in you and some dominion over you. . . ." He then prays for the exorcists "that they may have the power to command spirits, to cast forth from the bodies of those who are obsessed demons with every kind of wickedness and deceit." It was clear that the exorcist was ordained "to cast out demons."

It was noted that a parish priest must consult a bishop and get his authorization before performing an exorcism.

The character of the individual exorcist was also important. He had to be mature, "humble, of blameless life, courageous," a man of "scholarship and learning." [1]

And, most important, the presence of true possession must exist before exorcism could be employed. In other words, all other possibilities, such as "melancholia and any other illness" must be ruled out.[2] Symptoms that many considered to be signs of the presence of a demon were numerous: hysteria, dual personality, some forms of epilepsy, deep or prolonged sleep, intestinal pain, blasphemy, aggressiveness. All these, though often accepted as signs of possession, could be symptoms of mental or physical disorders.

The *Rituale Romanum* set down three specific signs of possession: "use or understanding of an unknown tongue; knowledge of distant or hidden facts; and exhibitions of physical powers exceeding the age or condition of the subject." [3] This latter condition was rather vague, and was open to various interpretations. One modern student of exorcism ponders this prerequisite in relation to unusual powers of levitation. He quotes an old case told to him by a French Catholic priest. One of the priest's missionairies was present at an exorcism, and reported the following:

> I took it upon myself, during an exorcism, to command the demon, in Latin, to carry [the possessed] to the ceiling

of the church, feet first and head downward. His whole body at once became rigid, and as if all his limbs had lost their power, he was dragged from the middle of the church to a pillar; there, with feet joined, and his back against the pillar, and without using his hands, he was carried in the twinkling of an eye to the ceiling, like a weight drawn violently upward, but without apparent means. Suspended from the ceiling, feet up, head downward . . . I left him there in the air for more than half an hour, and not having resolution enough to keep him there any longer, and not a little frightened myself at what I saw, I commanded [the spirit] to bring him back to my feet without doing him any hurt. . . . He was returned to me at once, like a bag of dirty linen, unharmed." [4]

If this story were true, certainly no natural cause could explain it. And if scientists could not explain it, the theologians could attribute it to the intervention of the devil.

The three criterion of the *Rituale* are still basically in force today. The individual churchman must make the decision whether true possession exists or not. According to the *Rituale,* the exorcism itself should preferably take place in a church and "no crowd of gazers" should assemble there "out of mere curiosity."

The exorcist is cautioned to use the words of the Church, not his own, and "all idle and impertinent questioning of the demon is to be avoided, nor should the evil spirit be allowed to speak at length unchecked and unrebuked."

The *Rituale* outlined the specific prayers and wording of the Church exorcism, in which the priest urges—in the name of Jesus Christ—the devil to depart the possessed. The rites were to be repeated until "the possessed person be entirely set free." [5]

After it had been established to the best of the churchman's ability that an individual was truly possessed, the exorcism would be performed according to the *Rituale Romanum*. The rite, itself, was divided into five parts: prayer; then exorcism; prayer again; exorcism again; and then prayer again, this time interrupted in various places by readings from the Scriptures. The exorcism was addressed to the demon. The prayer was to the possessed, to help him or her desire to be rid of the devil, and reinforce the idea that divine power was trying to help the person. Exorcisms and prayers were to be accompanied by various rites and objects of the Church: the signs of the cross, the layings on of hands, holy water, and the sacraments. The exorcist was told in detail what language to use.[6]

Later (1626) a *Manuale Exorcismorum* went into detail as to how exorcisms should be carried out. It gave a number of formulas for the rites. One of them alone covered nearly forty pages.[7]

In spite of the Church's attempt to systematize the rites and uses of exorcism, irregularities continued. The most troubling were cases of fake misdiagnosed possession. Many of these were, of course, closely tied to witchcraft, still very much in the popular mind.

One day in Staffordshire, England, a young boy came home ill from school. He vomited pins and feathers and wool, and his urine turned black. His parents were deeply concerned, particularly when the boy said he must have been bewitched by an old woman who had been angered because she said he was rude to her. The boy's parents sought the aid of their Catholic priest. He came to the house and said many prayers and anointed the boy with holy water. The priest said he had driven the devils—three of them—out of the boy. However, these devils returned, although they now seemed to come back only when there were Protestants present. Then the boy would shout and yell. The old woman was arrested and tried as a witch, but she was found not guilty. The matter did not stop there. Civil authorities suspected there was more involved than met the eye. They brought in doctors to examine the boy for signs of bewitchment. One doctor, on peeking through a keyhole, saw the boy putting ink into the chamber pot to make his urine black.

It finally was revealed that the Catholic priests had planned the stunt so that they might show off the power of their Church in driving out demons. The boy had been carried away in the excitement and the attention and had carried the game too far.[8]

But not all cases of possession, by far, can be ascribed to trickery or epilepsy. During the early seventeenth century there was an epidemic of possessed nuns in convents throughout Europe. The most famous of these cases is one which occurred at the Ursuline Convent at Loudun, France.

In 1617, Urbain Grandier, a handsome young priest, was appointed vicar of Saint-Pierre du Marché, at Loudun. He had gained quite a reputation as a romancer of ladies, much to the chagrin of the various holy fathers at Loudun. He also had made political enemies in France. Thus he was well known to the nuns at the convent. Suddenly—it seemed—the nuns became possessed. First to be afflicted was the superior, Sister Jeanne des Anges, who had fits. She saw phantoms in the cloister, heard strange voices. Soon some of the other nuns became possessed. Pierre Barré, a simple, sincere priest, was called in to perform the formal exorcism ritual. As he began the rites Sister Jeanne des Anges thrashed about. She "fell into fearful paroxysms, her face seemed to alter to that of a grinning fiend, a circumstance which filled the bystanders with no ordinary fear; her tongue, black and swollen, was thrust from her parched and cracking lips; her skin dripped with sweat; her limbs . . . writhed and twisted in all directions; her body ballooned to an immense size." [9]

Sister Jeanne spoke in a harsh voice not her own, saying that two devils possessed her. During the exorcisms, which lasted over a period of many months, both she and the many other nuns who were now possessed accused Urbain Grandier of having bewitched them. There was much publicity about the case; the court examined and reexamined the nuns, as did the priests and doctors. Grandier was questioned time after time, and he came under grave suspicion when a "heretical document" was discovered at his house. Grandier was finally arrested and thrown into prison on November 30, 1633. He was tried on August 18, 1634, and condemned to the stake. His crime was "of magic, of injuries and possessions practiced upon the persons of several Ursuline nuns of this town of Loudun, as well as upon other seculars." [10]

After the death sentence was carried out, there was some surprise to find that the nuns were still possessed.

Several of the other exorcists who had been called in also suffered severely by being involved with the nuns.

Fathers Tranquille and Lactance performed the exorcism rites time after time before crowds in the church. They finally became ill, being "beset by the very demons they had helped to evoke,"[11] and died. After their deaths Father Jean-Pierre Surin joined the exorcists at the convent. He was a very straitlaced person, and the constant talk of the nuns about their fantasies was very distressing to him.

He was successful in driving out one of the devils on January 7, 1636, and the other, the devil of blasphemy, on October 15, when he and Sister Jeanne met at the tomb of a saint in Annecy. But Surin also suffered sorely, afflicted with symptoms of possession, and was ill for many years. It was 1660 before he became calm and could resume his ministerial duties without thoughts of devils.[12]

Author Aldous Huxley was to write hundreds of years later about the Devils of Loudun: "Left to themselves such devils as remained soon took their leave. . . . The long orgy was at an end. If there had been no exorcists, it would never have begun."[13]

A case of possession occurred in Austria which was to become celebrated in folk tale and song, and centuries later caught the attention of the psychoanalyst Sigmund Freud.

Balladeers went about the countryside singing about the "painter boy" who was "freed of a pact signed in his own blood miraculously at Mariazell."

Johann Christoph Haizmann was an artist who was employed at Pottenbrunn Castle. He had been born in Bavaria and at an early age had been left, by the death of a parent, to shift for himself.

In 1677, the year of this tale, he was twenty-five years old. One Sunday while in church he suffered convulsions, which continued for several days. Haizmann went to the village priest, Father Leopold Braun, and told him the strange story of "his pact with the devil."

Nine years earlier, Johann, with no job and little money, was in the nearby forest. The devil came to him and said he would help him, if in nine years he would give himself over to the devil "body and soul." The pact had been written in blood. The nine years were almost up. On September 24, said Haizmann, the exact anniversary of the meeting, the devil would come to claim him. The painter wanted to break the pact and be freed from the devil.

Father Braun listened sympathetically. He wrote a letter to the Father Superior of the monastery at Mariazell, asking for his help. Haizmann went to Mariazell and there the monks prepared to perform an exorcism over the frightened painter.

The exorcism, conducted by Father Sebastian Meitinger, helped by three other monks, took place near midnight on September 8. It was declared to be successful. The painter was released from the pact with the devil. Haizmann then left the monastery and went to his sister's house in Vienna. But instead of finding peace there he was plagued with the most terrifying visions and hallucinations. Haizmann then recalled there had been two pacts with the devil, the first written in black ink, and the second in blood. The devil still had the second one. Haizmann was certain that Satan could come and call for him at any moment. So the painter went back to Mariazell, where further exorcism was performed over him. Finally, on May 9, 1678, his pact with the devil was broken. The actual "document" was found, on the steps of the church altar, torn into four pieces and rolled into a ball.

After this ordeal, Haizmann decided to take up the life of a monk. In the winter of 1681 he joined the Order of the Brothers Hospitaller in Vienna. He died in 1700 in another monastery in Bohemia, leaving several paintings depicting his emotional involvement with the devil. These attracted the interest of Sigmund Freud in his studies of the case two centuries later.

The first painting invoked the mood of the first encounter with the devil in the forest. It showed the devil in the guise of a respectable citizen, in hat and coat, and with well-trimmed beard. The next painting of the devil shows him in "blood covered brownish red, partly naked, horned, with birdlike claws instead of feet, and with two rows of breasts, one above the other. He also has a long tail. . . ." In later paintings the devil becomes more and more sinister. The last painting shows him as "a satanic dragon figure, and truly terrifying."

Freud said Haizmann's pact with the devil was a "neurotic phantasy . . ." and Haizmann was "this poor devil" himself. "His road took him from his father, by way of the devil as Substitute Father, back to the devout Fathers." [14]

Although many contemporary reports were preserved on his case, along with Haizmann's paintings (as well as a diary he kept between the two exorcisms), there was no record of the actual exorcisms performed.

Exorcism took many forms. Sometimes it was a simple

prayer, sometimes it was a more elaborate ritual as prescribed by the *Rituale Romanum.*

One system of exorcism of the seventeenth century was used by the Jesuits, and was common in the Spanish Inquisition. Its purpose was to drive the demons from a place, rather than a person. Part of it read:

> I adjure thee, O serpent of old, by the Judge of the living and the dead; by the Creator of the world who hath power to cast into hell, that thou depart forthwith from this house. He that commands thee, accursed demon, is He that commanded the winds, and the sea and the storm. He that commands thee is He that ordered thee to be hurled down from the height of heaven into the lower parts of the earth. He that commands thee is He that bade thee depart from Him. Hearken, then, Satan, and fear. Get thee gone, vanquished and cowed, when thou art bidden in the name of our Lord Jesus Christ who will come to judge the living and the dead and all the world by fire. Amen.[15]

As has been noted, not all exorcisms were carried out in a church, or by the use of formal religious languages. This was especially true in cases where local priests or pastors were involved.

By the eighteenth century it was well established that one of the signs of possession was that the demon or evil spirit spoke out through the lips of the possessed. The voice never was the person's natural one, rather it was the harsh, rough voice of a demon. Thus the exorcist was able to converse with the devil.

On the evening of December 14, 1714, the pastor of a Catholic church in a little town in Swabia, Germany, heard a rumor that two possessed women had been brought to the workhouse. He decided to go and discover the truth of the matter. After he saw the women, he went back to his church, sat down and wrote the bishop:

> After . . . the paroxysm began in one of the possessed women and Satan abruptly hurled this invective at me by her mouth: "Silly fool, what are you doing in this workhouse? You'll get lice here," I made him this answer: "By the blood, the wounds and the martyrdom of Jesus Christ, thou shalt be vanquished and expelled!" Thereupon he foamed with rage and shouted: "If we had the devil's power we would turn earth and heaven upside down. . . . What God doesn't want is ours!"

The next day the pastor had the possessed woman brought to his church, and he began an exorcism. He sang songs, and read passages from the Bible. As he did these things, the devil in the woman protested, and asked him to please finish with the rites. It complained—through the mouth of the woman—"Won't you soon have done?"

The pastor replied: "When it is enough for God it will be enough for thee, demon!"

Then the devil shouted again: "How dost thou oppress, how dost thou torment me! If only I had been wise enough not to enter thy church!"

The demon threatened to make the woman suffer with it, calling her its "creature."

The pastor spoke up angrily: "Demon! The creature is not thine but God's! That which is thine is filth and unclean things, hell and damnation to all eternity!"

The pastor continued to rail against the demon, who at last cried out, "Oh, I burn, I burn! Oh, what torture! What torture!"

All this time the devil treated the woman dreadfully.

It "howled through her mouth in a frightful manner and threw her to the ground so rigid, so insensible that she became as cold as ice and lay as dead, at which time we could not perceive the slightest breath until at last with God's help she came to herself."

When the woman had recovered, she was not able to remember anything at all about what had happened.[16]

THE NINETEENTH CENTURY

The peak of obsession with witchcraft had long since passed by the beginning of the nineteenth century. Yet peoples in diverse parts of the world continued to cling to belief in witches, black magic, and evil spirits, so there was still a demand for exorcism.

In England the Protestant Church did not at this time recognize demon-possession or exorcism. Yet many people felt the need of the services of an exorcist, and they often called upon the Catholic priests in their area for such services.

One such occasion occurred in the spring of 1815 when a young married woman living in the countryside near Worcestershire fell ill. Doctor after doctor went to see the ailing woman, but none could diagnose her disease, and all said they were helpless to cure her.

She was in a state of hysteria. She raved of evil spirits who were attacking her; how they would not leave her alone, day or night. The woman's sister blamed a rejected lover who had vowed his revenge. She knew he had hired a noted wizard of Worcestershire expressly to do the family harm.

Since the doctors were helpless, the local Church of England vicar went to visit the sick woman. Although he prayed with her, she showed no signs of improvement. One day the Catholic nurse who was in attendance became extremely distressed by the ravings of the woman. The nurse went to the Roman Catholic church and filled a bottle with holy water.

On returning to the house, the nurse went to the patient's room and sprinkled the holy water about the room and on the bed. A few drops fell on the woman, who suddenly cried out: "You have scalded me, scalded me! You have scalded me!"

The nurse soothed her for a few moments, and the young woman quieted down and fell into a peaceful sleep. For two days she was much better, neither crying nor shouting, but then on the third day she was attacked by violent convulsions. Her family decided that only an exorcist could help her. They sought the services of Catholic Father Edward Peach of the Midland District.

When Father Peach arrived at the house he found the woman in a dreadful state. Two women and the husband were holding her down on the bed. She struggled so hard that in a few minutes she fell back on the bed in exhaustion.

Father Peach told the others to leave the room. He then began a long quiet talk with the woman. After some discussion, Father Peach concluded that there was no natural cause for her illness, and that she was truly diabolically possessed. He also discovered that she had never been baptized.

There, Father Peach thought, lay the answer. He ordered

the preparations made quickly, and began the baptism. As the water touched the woman, she trembled, and a look of pain crossed her face. (She later told Father Peach that the water had been "boiling.") At the end of the baptism she was relaxed, but weak. She gained strength over the next few days and recovered completely. Never again was she plagued by any more symptoms of her illness.[1]

So demonic possession and exorcism of devils continued as part of the life of Western Europe in the nineteenth century.

These beliefs also existed elsewhere.

In nineteenth-century Russia an orthodox priest named Father Johann of Kronstadt was revered through the countryside, and regarded as a saint by many, because of his special powers of exorcism. People came to Saint Petersburg from miles around to seek the cures his prayers could bring.

According to a contemporary report in the Saint Petersburg *Gazette,* one day the police were notified that a woman who had recently arrived in the city was behaving in a very strange fashion. Whenever the church bells rang out, wherever she might be, she fell to the ground, began to shriek in a wild voice and soon was covered with perspiration. If a church procession went by the same thing happened to her. She caused no other disturbance, so the police put her down as a "crackpot" and left her alone.

Her erratic behavior continued for three years. Finally her family thought to seek the help of Father Johann of Kronstadt.

The woman was taken to Father Johann's church in Saint

Petersburg, where the priest was conducting his services. The congregation was rising to receive communion, and she was brought to the railing. Suddenly she was overcome with a "fit." She screamed, tore at her face, and writhed on the floor. Three men had to hold her down.

Father Johann gently placed his hand on her, looked deeply into her eyes, and said in a loud voice: "In the name of Our Lord Jesus Christ I command thee, Satan, to come forth!

"Come forth, and come quickly!"

The congregation fell silent as the priest spoke the words over and over again.

Finally the woman let out a few cries. From her lips came the words: "I am coming forth immediately!"

Then she closed her eyes and swayed into the priest's arms. He told her to open her eyes, which she did.

He told her to cross herself. She found it difficult to make the first sign, but the others came more easily. Eventually she gained some composure, and the priest turned to those around her and said: "Leave her, she is now completely cured!"

Father Johann offered her holy communion, which she accepted. She left the church, and never again did she suffer an attack.[2]

In Japan belief in possession was also widespread, but it was not possession by the devil known to the Western world. Possession in Japan was most often by animals whose spirits were said to enter human bodies. Foxes were the animals most commonly charged with invading a human body, but dogs, cats, monkeys, badgers, snakes, and other creatures were also able to do this.

Exorcism was such a necessary adjunct to the lives of the Japanese, that the main activity of one religious sect, the Nichiren, was exorcism.

The Nichiren maintained a famous temple in a village near Tokyo. Here hundreds of possessed persons gathered to be exorcised from their particular possessors.

A German professor of medicine, who was at the University of Tokyo, recorded details about a number of possession cases in Japan.

Typical of these cases was one involving a young girl who fell ill, with the doctors unable to do anything. She was literally wasting away, and after some weeks her family thought it necessary to summon a noted exorcist of the Nichiren sect. The exorcist came, and performed a formal exorcism, but the spirit—in this case a fox—would not leave the girl's body. The fox announced (in her voice) that it was too clever to be taken in by any religious ceremonies.

But it did say it would leave the girl's body if a good feast was prepared for it. The exorcist asked what the fox desired, and it replied that on a certain day, at the special temple for the foxes, twelve kilometers away, at four o'clock, a grand meal should be laid out.

It demanded rice cooked in a special way, cheese cooked with beans, a hundred roast mice, and many plates of vegetables. (These were the favorite dishes of magic foxes.)

If the feast were prepared as the spirit had demanded, it would leave the girl at the proper time. But if not— never!

A many-eyed
Japanese demon
possesses a young man.

THE NINETEENTH CENTURY | 51

The food was all cooked and arranged. It was brought to the foxes' temple at four o'clock on the prescribed day. At the very moment that the table was set, the sick girl sighed, and cried out: "He has gone!"

The exorcist had cured the possession.[3]

Japanese exorcists knew other methods to drive out the foxes. If a professional exorcist was not available, an ordinary person would threaten the fox with a sharp weapon and the evil spirit was likely to disappear. A Samurai father with a possessed daughter tied her to a pillar, ran up to her with a drawn sword, and cried out: "Wicked spirit, if thou dost not forthwith leave this child I will kill you both!"

The fox fled immediately and the girl was cured.[4]

Animals were also said to possess humans in the Malay Peninsula. One account of an exorcism involved a sick man and a tiger.

The exorcist, a Malay medicine man, performed a long traditional exorcism over the patient who was lying on the floor on a mat.

Around the sick man were grouped a number of villagers shaking tambourines and beating drums. Water jars were stacked around the patient's body. A kettle of raw rice with palm fronds alongside stood by the exorcist's hand. A jar of sweet oil stood at his feet. In his belt he carried a short dagger.

First the exorcist threw incense on the coals of a fire. Then, with motions as if he were washing his body, he drew the smoke of the incense about him. Next he inhaled the smoke and lay down on the floor, covering his face with his sarong.

The exorcist rolled about on the ground, then sat upright facing a tambourine player. After turning to face a number of water jars, he changed his clothes, putting on a new white jacket and head cloth, then took three silver twenty-cent pieces, spoke a charm over them, and dropped them into a water jar.

He said charms over several handfuls of rice and scattered these around the row of jars. Next he took palm fronds and placed them in the three jars of water, then plunged a dagger into each of the three fronds (where it was suspected that the hostile spirits were lurking, having been drawn out previously by invocation).

Then the exorcist took another palm frond, put oil on it, and after placing it on the patient's chest, brushed it down the sick man's body until the feet.

Then he beat the ground with the palm until he fell back on the floor exhausted.

After a time the exorcist got up on all fours and did imaginary combat with the tiger spirit who had now gone from the sick man's body into the exorcist's. The exorcist growled, and then "slowly licked over, as a tigress would lick its cub, the all but naked body of the patient." Then the exorcist pierced his own arm with the dagger and drew blood. Again he did combat with the tiger, and beat about with a palm. With convulsive twitchings the exorcist "returned to consciousness and sat up, and the ceremony was over."[5]

In China, too, animals were said to be able to possess a person. Here the fox, wolf, and tiger were feared the most. The fox was considered the most powerful of all. But in addition to animal spirits, other demons were responsible, people thought, for causing illness. So the exorcist in China too, was an important man, and had been for hundreds of years.

John L. Nevius, a Christian missionary who lived in China in the nineteenth century, followed many cases of possession.

One involved the family of a man named Chang who lived in a small village. The women of the household said a demon came into the house and had told them it wanted to be worshipped, to have a shrine within the home. Chang did not believe the story and he refused the request. But then one of the women began to act very erratically, and strange things began happening. Fires broke out in the house, without any visible cause. Dishes broke. Furniture moved about. Food and clothing disappeared. Chang had heard that the Christians were never bothered by evil spirits, so he sought the help of a woman named Fung. She came to the house and exorcised the demon. The household returned to normal for a few days.

But it began again and the family again had to seek help. This time the demon was even more destructive. A woman named Liu came and found one of the daughters-in-law lying on the bed, tossing about wildly. She was "under the influence of the demon and demanded wine, which she drank in large quantities." Mrs. Liu held an informal exorcism over this family member and another woman who had threatened to drown or hang herself.

After the exorcism the fowl and the pigs in the yard suddenly made a huge commotion and ran about helter-skelter. That convinced the family that the devil had left them and "had taken possession of the fowl and the swine."[6]

The devil was very helpful to the Christian missionaries in converting the Chinese as it became generally accepted that Christians were protected by their God from possession.

In 1862 a French missionary, Monsignor Anouil, wrote in a letter back to France about the devil and exorcism:

> Would you believe it? The villages have been converted! The devil is furious and is playing all sorts of tricks. During the fortnight's preaching which I have just completed there have been five or six cases of possession. Our catechumens with holy water drive out the devils and cure the sick. I have seen some marvelous things. The devil is a great help to me in converting the heathen; as in the time of Our Lord, although the Father of Lies he cannot help speaking the truth. For instance, one poor possessed man executed innumerable contortions and shrieked aloud: "Why dost thou preach the true religion? I cannot bear to have my disciples taken away by thee." "What is thy name?" asked the catechist. After some refusals, "I am the envoy of Lucifer."
>
> "How many are you?"
>
> "We are twenty-two."
>
> Holy water and the sign of the cross delivered this demoniac.[7]

One French case of possession was that of Hélène-Joséphine Poirier. She was born in the village of Coullons in the Loire district. As a young girl Hélène was adept at needlework, and was apprenticed to a dressmaker. She was industrious, and seemed happy and well adjusted. But on the night of March 25, 1850, the fifteen-year-old girl had a strange experience. She was awakened from sleep in her small attic room by a number of sharp raps on the walls. The rapping grew louder and louder. Hélène awakened her parents, and they all went to her room. The rappings were still audible, but no one could discover the source of the commotion.

The family soon forgot the incident. But several months later when Hélène was at home she suddenly fell to the ground, as though some one had roughly pushed her. She got up but fell down again. Her parents feared that she had experienced an epileptic fit or some other type of attack. They took her to the local doctor, Dr. Azéma, but he could find nothing physically wrong. He told her, "Nobody here but the priest can cure you."

From that time on Hélène's condition worsened: She had spasms and painful trances, which continued for thirteen years. Finally everyone decided that the illness must have a supernatural origin. The family sought the help of the Archdeacon of Orleans, the Abbé Bougaud. After examining her, the Abbé decided that she should be taken to the bishop, Monsignor Dupanloup. Hélène was taken to a convent to await her appointment. But then came a round of misunderstandings. A doctor called at the convent. He examined the young woman, and reported to the mother superior and the bishop that in his opinion Hélène was simply mad and should be sent home. Hélène did go home, in disappointment, for she still was suffering greatly.

Almost a year passed. Her condition remained the same. Then one day the bishop went to Coullons on business matters, and agreed to see Hélène. This visit caused him to completely revise his first thoughts about the girl. He was convinced that there was a supernatural cause for her symptoms. The Archdeacon of Orleans again visited Hélène and came to the same conclusion.

By March of 1868 it seemed obvious to all that Hélène

was possessed. Fits would seize her; she would fall to the ground, and in a deep hoarse voice shout out blasphemies. She gnashed her teeth and foamed at the mouth if the name of Jesus was mentioned in her presence. She went into wild rages, and waved her arms about and howled. Various clergymen tried to help her. They questioned her in Latin, and she answered the questions at length and with great ease—in Latin. The case received much publicity and through the clerical hierarchy was brought to the attention of Pope Pius IX in Rome. He expressed the greatest of sympathy for Hélène, and sent a message to the clergy cautioning "avoidance of curiosity or advertisement."

A priest continued to examine Hélène, hoping to discover the forces that were causing her such suffering. In February 1869 she was again questioned by a number of priests, and gave them much information about cults of Satanists, information to which a woman living in a small village in France would have no access. She spoke of the Satanic bands in Paris, Rome, and Tours, and of the "devil-worshippers" at Toulouse. She described in great detail the meetings of the Satanists with the devil in those places. (The priests said the facts she gave them were true.)

Finally the bishop arranged for Hélène to be taken to Orleans to be examined—and exorcised.

The questioning was done by priests who were theological experts. As Hélène sat before them she had painful cramps and spasms. She howled and writhed. But the priests persisted, and tried to comfort her. They spoke to her in both Latin and Greek of religious matters, and she answered fluently and knowledgeably in both languages. The bishop came into the questioning sessions several days later, and he, too, was amazed at Hélène's ability to speak in languages she did not know, and with such sophistication. He immediately ordered his director, a professor at the seminary, to conduct the exorcisms for Hélène.

The exorcism held in April 1869 proved most difficult. Two nuns and another woman had to hold Hélène. She cried, she foamed at the mouth, she cursed God, she broke free and threw chairs and furniture. The rites were conducted once a day for five days. On the last day Hélène was more violent than usual, but finally was restrained. Then suddenly, with a terrible yell, repeated twice, she relaxed and seemed as though asleep. Then she awoke, calm and composed. It had been nineteen years since she had heard the rappings on her bedroom wall!

The exorcism was a success.

For four months Hélène seemed normal. Then she became involved in trying to help convert to the Catholic religion a famous army general of the day, a man named Ducrot. Her symptoms returned. This time, because the case was so celebrated, she was taken to Lourdes for exorcism in September 1875, and the prayers of fifteen thousand pilgrims who had gathered there exorcised the evil spirits from her. Although she was to live forty more years, she was never possessed again.[8]

The Murrell case, a completely different type of exorcism, took place in a small English village about forty miles (64 km) from London. James Murrell was a small man, with bright blue eyes and a ruddy complexion. He had been a shoemaker in the village of Hadleigh, South Essex, until he gave up that profession to become a magician. His little cottage on a narrow lane was filled with drying herbs that hung from the ceiling. His wooden chest contained books on magic.

Murrell was a man of many abilities. He could trace lost property, he could summon the good angels, or he could exorcise demons—all for a fee. Murrell's witchcraft is still legendary today in Hadleigh. Here is his story:

Sometime during the 1850 harvest season a young girl went into a barn after the harvesters had left for the day. She found an old gypsy there, and rudely ordered her to get out. The gypsy reluctantly left the barn, but muttered, "You'll be sorry for this, my girl."

Just after those words were spoken, the girl suffered a fit. She ran about on all fours, barked like a dog, and mewed like a cat. Her family suspected witchcraft after hearing about the gypsy. They called in the wizard Murrell. He immediately recognized the case as one of witchcraft.

Murrell took some of the girl's urine, and blended it with blood, special herbs, and pins. He put this mixture into a bottle and heated it on a fire. The living room of the house was darkened, all lights put out, and the doors were locked. Murrell told the family to keep silent or the spell to drive the demon out of the girl would be broken.

Shortly, Murrell and the family heard footsteps outside the door, then a rapid and loud knocking. At the same time, the voice of an old woman cried out:

"For God's sake, stop. You're killing me."

At that second the bottle exploded. The voice outside disappeared. From that very moment the ailing girl recovered. And, so the legend goes, the next morning "the body of an old gypsy woman covered with dreadful burns was discovered in the road three miles away." [9]

A stone column stands thirty feet (9 m) high in the town of Illfurt in Alsace, that often disputed territory between France and Germany. The inscription on this monument commemorates, in Latin, the "liberation of possession" of Theobald and Joseph Burner, in 1869.

These strange, terrifying cases involved the possession of two young boys. Theobald was ten and Joseph nearly eight when their peculiar activities began. Parish records give the details:

Lying on their backs, the boys would suddenly spin around like tops. When in bed they turned their faces to the wall and painted pictures of the devil on it. Supposedly they could levitate: "While sitting on a chair, boy and chair were at times lifted into the air, and then dropped in such a way that the boy was flung into one corner of the room, and the chair into the opposite corner. . . ." They had convulsions, they vomited "foam, feathers, and seaweed." Sometimes the boys did not speak for days, but just glared and slobbered. Other times they shouted and waved their arms wildly. When they spoke their voices were harsh and ugly. They would swear and shriek, and blaspheme.

"When a clergyman or pious Catholic visited the house the possessed children crawled hastily under a table or bed or jumped out the window." But when "a mediocre Christian" was in the house, the boys, according to the parish report, "showed great delight," and said of the visitor: "That is one of ours. They should all be like that!"

Dr. Levy from a nearby town was called in to examine the boys, but he had no idea of what was causing such distressing actions. Other doctors were summoned, but were no more successful. The church authorities of the town finally came to believe that the boys were possessed, according to the standards set forth in the *Rituale Romanum*. One of the convincing aspects was that the boys, even when shouting and swearing, answered with correct grammar questions put to them, and spoke fluently in French, Latin, English, and even in different dialects of Spanish and Italian. These languages could not have been known by the boys, for they had not been exposed to them. Neither had any more than the ordinary education of the local elementary school. This ability to speak in foreign languages was considered to be one of the real signs of diabolic possession.

The church and town authorities decided that the evil spirits had to be exorcised from the boys. Theobald was taken first for his exorcism to an institution in Schiltigheim. According to the records, "the devil was silent for three days." On the fourth day it spoke in a voice that reminded the nun on duty of "a calf being strangled." The devil said: "Here I am. And I am in a fury." When asked by the nun who he was, the devil replied: "I am the Lord of Darkness."

The boy shouted and tore his clothes, and broke everything that he could touch. He was finally tied up.[10]

The exorcism itself was held in the church. It was truly a battle: Theobald, yelling and shouting, was held by several abbés and the very hefty gardener. The boy struggled to break free. His face grew beet red. He closed his eyes as the froth from his mouth fell to the floor. Then the prayers and the ritual began. Theobald kept screaming, but the exorcist remained calm and continued with the ritual until the end.

But Theobald remained unchanged. The churchmen decided to try the exorcism again the next day.

The following day Theobald was put in a straitjacket, and three guards stood over him as he was strapped into a red armchair. Again he did the same things: he roared in a hoarse voice and fought to be free, while his face turned scarlet and the foam dripped from his lips.

The exorcism began. The priest held the crucifix and other religious statues in front of the boy and called the demon.

"Unclean spirit, disappear before the face of the Immaculate Conception! She commands! Thou must obey! Thou must depart!"

The priest's assistants were on their knees reciting prayers. Suddenly Theobald let out a hideous, painful screech. He had one sharp convulsion, and then he slumped over. For an hour he lay still. Then he awoke, quietly looked around him, and spoke:

"Where am I?"

Abbé Schrantzer said to him: "Do you not know me?"

"No, Father," said Theobald, "I do not." [11]

The exorcism was a success. Theobald was tired but happy, and, most important, calm. No longer was he possessed by the devil. In a few days he went home and never had any recollection of those four dreadful years that he had suffered, nor of the exorcism that had been performed over him.

Joseph, meanwhile, continued to exhibit the same erratic behavior. He was taken, in October 1869, to the little chapel of the cemetery near Illfurt for his exorcism. Fewer than a dozen people were present—his parents, the clergy, and a professor.

The Abbé Charles Brey said the mass, and then began the ritual. The prayers and adjurations to the devil went on for three hours. Nothing happened. Some of those present became discouraged and went away. The priest, however, was steadfast and full of hope. Finally, the young boy, who had been struggling and screaming, let out a long piercing roar and fell back in a faint.

Joseph lay still for a few moments. Then he sat up, opened his eyes, and the same question was on his lips as had been on his brother's.

He was surprised to find himself in the chapel with strangers gathered about him.[12]

Again exorcism had been successful. Joseph's parents took him home where he resumed his life as a normal boy and grew into a respected man.

The Church had put the cases down as true possession, according to the knowledge afforded them at the time, by Church standards. Present-day students of the cases have wondered whether, in light of today's knowledge and experience in mental illness and diseases such as epilepsy, such boys would be called "possessed." [12] For although "cured," both boys had died young, Theobald at sixteen and Joseph, at twenty-five. The deaths were called "normal," but who was to know?

Visitors to the Middle East in the nineteenth century sometimes brought back first-hand accounts of possession and exorcism.

In Cairo a German visitor met a carriage-load of persons returning from a Zar ceremony. The Zar is a particular spirit that takes over a person, usually a woman. Therefore, both men and women become Zar doctors. Many Zar cults protect the people against the Zar. In Cairo were many sanctuaries where regular exorcism of the Zar was undertaken; those more affluent had the Zar exorcisms performed in their homes.

As in the Christian churches, there were many different forms of exorcism. A Zar ceremony was not always designed to drive the Zar spirit out, but rather to placate it for a time.

In order for the Zar to completely disappear, the exorcists drew out the evil spirit and substituted a benevolent Zar into the patient. The original Zar was transported to a bush or tree in the countryside, where it could pounce upon some other unsuspecting person!

The duration of the exorcism varied. If the patient was wealthy the ceremony could be long, lasting from three to seven nights. The exorcist (called *shecha* or *schechah*) and the onlookers spent the last night in the patient's home. Exorcisms for the less affluent were held in the sanctuaries and lasted only a few hours.[13]

What exactly were the Zar cults and ceremonies? Possession by the Zar was common in nineteenth-century Mecca. It had many of the overtones of psychiatric treatment among some classes in the twentieth century. Apparently the suffering was not as serious as in other possession cases. In fact, it seemed an "in" thing for women.

Women in Mecca, brought up on talk of "Zar," accepted it as something natural. They were told that ailments were caused by the Zar, who also dominated the will of the person. Sometimes, however, possession *could* be violent. A woman could be thrown to the ground suffering from convulsions.

A patient might grow wild and have fits. Then the men wanted to call in doctors and resort to medicines, or to have a religious exorcism. The women around the patient, however, insisted on calling in the *Shechah-ez-Zar*. The *shechah* did not question the patient herself, but the Zar who inhabited her body.[14] This aspect was much like the European form of exorcism.

Sometimes the *shechah* spoke in an ordinary language and everyone present understood her. Other times she spoke a Zar language which they did not.

> On the reiterated injunction of the *shechah* the Zar declares himself ready to depart on a certain day with the usual ceremonies, if in the interim certain stipulations have been fulfilled. He demands a new and beautiful garment, gold or silver trinkets. As he himself is hidden from all human perception, nothing can be done except carry out his wish and make gifts of the specified objects to the sick body which he inhabits. On the day when the departure is to take place the patient's female friends, invited for the purpose, come in the afternoon or evening and are offered coffee or sometimes a concert of flutes. . . . The patient puts on the clothing demanded by the Zar. . . . The *shechah* handles the body of the possessed according to the rules of her art. [Sometimes] a lamb is sacrificed and the forehead and other parts of the body of the possessed are smeared with its blood. . . . [T]he possessed must dance, sway her body or else faint and this is the moment when the muttering *shechah* declares that the Zar has departed.[15]

Another German visitor in the Middle East described

his encounters with the followers of the Zar belief, which were similar to those found in Mecca.

> ... [A] crowd of women and girls stream into the house of the patient and are offered *busa,* the half-fermented Arab beer ... together with sheep's tripe. Then they sing, beat cymbals and dance the Zar-dance.... Soon some of them become possessed and leap around dancing madly. All this is under the direction of the *shechah*.... As soon as she and the others are in ecstasy, the somnambulist is questioned as to the means of curing the sickness. The remedy always consists in a plain silver finger-ring, thick, without stones, or more rarely in bracelets or anklets, and as soon as the greedy Zar is satisfied with this gift the malady disappears. Faith in success is so great that many sacrifice their last penny to obtain the silver ornament and meet the very considerable cost of entertaining the multitude of female guests.

During the dancing the women become so aroused that many times they "strike their faces, bang their heads against the walls, weep, howl, try to strangle themselves and are restrained only with difficulty." After getting the ring or some other piece of jewelry, "the possessed wipes the sweat from her and now talks composedly and reasonably as before...."[16]

A French visitor to Ethiopia wrote of the Abyssinians possessed by the "Zarr."

> ... The person who proclaims himself possessed rises in the middle of the night, rolls upon the ground and utters inarticulate cries. After one or two hours of contortions he is exhausted and remains lying as if inanimate....

The simple exorcism in a case such as this was for another person to take a hen and swing it around the head of the possessed, then throw the hen on the ground. If the hen died that meant that the Zarr had gone into the body of the fowl and caused it to die. If the hen lived, it meant that "the demon has resisted and has remained in the patient's body; another attempt must be made." [17]

The conditions described were not pretended. They were probably cases of delirium or ecstasy. Often that was the root of possession.

THE TWENTIETH CENTURY

Egypt in the twentieth century is becoming a modern country, and Cairo is in many ways a sophisticated city. Yet, the Zar are still known in present-day Egypt. The American writer Vivian Gornick spent some time in Egypt and visited a Zar session in Cairo.

It was held in "an adobe barn-type building in a Cairo alley, in a densely populated district between Midan Bab-el Louk and the Mosque of Sayeda Zeinab." The writer found there "about two hundred women dressed in black *milayehs* and the shapeless housedresses of the urban poor" who came "to exorcise their devils."

When she arrived, Gornick found the place in a frenzy.

> For eight hours at a time within the sweating walls of this barn, the drums beat insistently with a wild culminating beat that sends the women into a whirling, fainting frenzy of the dervish . . . skirts flying, head thrown back, eyes closed, limbs jerking to a final paroxysm of purging ecstasy. [The room] was alive with the gathered stench of sweat, fear and erotic exhaustion. . . .
>
> At the end of the session the women were relieved, re-

laxed, and even composed. One told the writer: "Yes, I come often to the Zar. I find it so refreshing." [1]

The Egyptian government is making efforts to stamp out such Zar meetings, but they have been unsuccessful. Zar is too deeply embedded in Egypt's culture to be gotten rid of easily.

That is also true in Ethiopia. In the 1950s, the Zar cult continued in full force in Gondar in the northern part of the country. It probably still does. Attempts have been made to conceal Zar from foreign visitors. The government says it has been completely suppressed in Addis Ababa, the capital.[2]

In Ethiopia symptoms of possession by Zar spirits include convulsions, sterility, proneness to accidents, and apathy. The healer, or exorcist, is also Zar-possessed, but he has "come to terms" with his spirit possession. When he is called to help a patient, his own Zar will possess him in a trance and try to lure the Zar out of the patient. It is an expensive process for the patient, who is pressured to join the Zar society, to "prevent any relapses."

The cult is really group therapy. It claims to help with "many psychological disturbances, ranging from frustrated status ambition to actual mental illness," and it has a certain role to play in the community. Since most of the patients are women, there is some resistance by husbands who "fear the sexual and economic emancipation of the wife." There is also some minor resistance from the priests who openly condemn the Zar cult, but do not take action against it, because many privately believe in the Zar themselves.[3]

This type of possession is far removed from possession by the Christian devil, as the story of Father Theophilus Riesinger indicates.

Father Theophilus was a member of an order of Capuchin monks, in Marathon, Wisconsin. He was an exorcist, who carefully examined each "possessed" person before he undertook a cure, since he felt that many symptoms might be those of hysteria. Even though he was a discriminating monk as far as the possessed were concerned, he claimed that by 1936 he had successfully exorcised twenty-two people. The case that received wide publicity, and was set down in a Roman Catholic booklet, published some years after the exorcism, involved a woman named Anna Ecklund.

Anna's first possession took place early in 1908, when she was still in her teens. This occurred because her Aunt Mina, commonly referred to in the neighborhood as a witch, had reportedly cast a spell on some herbs that were put in Anna's food. No one knew much about the first possession, but Father Theophilus "freed her from this possession" four years later.

In the past, "curses hurled against her by her wicked father" had thoroughly unbalanced Anna, and she was called "possessed." This situation lasted for the next sixteen years, long after her father and Aunt Mina died, until Father Theophilus came upon her case.

An interesting factor is that *Begone Satan*, the story of this exorcism, does not just include details of the rites and the prayers, but records the interrogations of the girl by the monk, Anna's actions through the ordeal, and Father Theophilus' talks with the many devils inside Anna.

Father Theophilus believed from the first that through his exorcism and the power of the Church that "we can force the devils to talk."

It would be too much to say that the Church booklet represented official Church policy, yet the account of the exorcism bore the imprimatur of Joseph F. Busch, Roman Catholic bishop of Saint Cloud, Minnesota, dated July 23, 1935.

Begone Satan was written originally in German by the Reverend Carl Vogl, and was later translated into English by the Reverend Celestine Kapsner. Thus, while not a policy document, it has the authenticity of Church sanction.

After Father Theophilus encountered Anna Ecklund he asked his bishop's permission to perform an exorcism. It was granted. But since the monk did not want publicity, he sought a place other than Anna's home town to carry out the exorcism. He asked Father Joseph Steiger of Earling, Iowa, some distance away, for permission to perform the exorcism there. Father Theophilus told Steiger how Anna had exhibited anti-Church activities, and warned him of the possible difficulties ahead. The bishop also warned Steiger that the devil might well want to take revenge upon him.

Under the circumstances Father Joseph was not enthusiastic about having an exorcism performed in his parish. But Father Theophilus went to the Franciscan convent in the area. The mother superior agreed, so Father Steiger reluctantly also agreed.

One day in August 1928 Anna Ecklund boarded the train for Earling. She was a bit disorderly on the train but that was as nothing compared to her greeting of the nuns who came to meet her. She shouted at them and tried to choke one of them, but they were strong enough to get her under control and take her to the convent. That was the beginning. It grew much worse in the days that were to follow.

When Anna discovered the food brought to her had been blessed, she flew into a rage and refused to eat. She made animal noises, purred like a cat, until unblessed food was brought.

The next morning the exorcism began. It was to continue for twenty-three days.

Anna flailed about, made more animal noises. Sometimes she was a lion, sometimes a cow, and sometimes a dog. She yelped and howled for hours. She hurled herself about. She cursed the Church. She vomited "unmentionable excrements" as many as ten to twenty times a day.

Shortly after Father Theophilus had begun the exorcism rite, Anna leaped from the bed on which she had been placed "and her body, carried through the air, landed high above the door of the room and clung to the wall with a tenacious grip. . . ."

Father Theophilus told the nuns and the guards to pull her down. "Real force had to be applied to her feet to bring her down from her high position on the wall. . . . It was through the powers of the evil spirit, who had taken possession of her body."

With all this commotion within the convent walls, there was no hope of keeping it quiet. The people of the village soon learned of the exorcism. It was the talk of the place.

As Father Theophilus was conversing with the devils within the girl, he heard many voices, some harsh, some human sounding, all coming from within the girl. One of the devils was Beelzebub. Another was Jacob, who had been Anna's father but was now "in hell," along with Aunt Mina, who had been his mistress. Jacob said he had given Anna to the devils.

Father Theophilus continued to interrogate the devils within Anna. She was coherent only a small part of the time. There was much yelling and thrashing about. From looking at Anna's physical appearance, it was obvious that she was suffering. The nuns suffered too. Some had to leave the room from time to time, exhausted. Father Joseph was upset, and it was said that the devilish voices coming from Anna taunted him, blaming him for letting the exorcism take place in his parish.

"You will have to suffer for all this," the devil reportedly told Steiger, and warned that on the coming Friday it would have revenge.

And on that Friday, while Father Joseph was driving back from visiting one of his parishioners, he did have an accident. Though he was unharmed, the car was ruined. When she next saw him, Anna yelled: "I certainly showed him up today! How about your new auto, that dandy car which was smashed to smithereens? It served you right!"

During these many days of exorcism, Father Joseph was even more visibly upset. Anna was coherent only part of the time. Everyone but Father Theophilus was becoming discouraged.

Between questions there were often tiresome long periods of silence. Other times when Father Theophilus sought the devils to answer his questions there was only "a ghastly bellowing, growling, and howling...."

Anna was clear-headed when she spoke in the morning, and apparently did not remember what had gone on during the exorcisms. At times when she was calm she spoke about the battle of good and evil spirits within her. She also had visions.

And then one evening, December 23, 1928, as in so many of the recorded exorcism cases, Anna suddenly fell on her bed and let out a piercing cry. She said, "Beelzebub, Judas, Jacob, Mina . . . hell—hell—hell—" Then she opened her eyes. She smiled. She said, "My Jesus, Mercy! Praised be Jesus Christ!"

The devils were exorcised from Anna Ecklund, and she returned home a normal woman.[4]

It is obvious that as cultures vary in different parts of the world, so do philosophies and beliefs. But too often we think in concepts of our own societies and express amazement at occurrences in other, foreign lands. In the United States in the twentieth century possession and exorcism are rare enough that they cause considerable comment when they come to public attention. Yet in a land such as India, spirit possession is widespread, and is accepted as an integral part of life.

In the late 1950s Stanley and Ruth Freed visited several small villages in north India to study spirit possession. They discovered that possession of a person by a spirit or a godling results in psychological illness, and these possessions are widespread.

One case of possession they witnessed concerned a fifteen-year-old bride, who was staying at her husband's home. The Freeds, the mother-in-law, and various relatives, along with the girl, called Daya, were all chatting in the sitting room. Daya was sewing, quiet and respectful as a new bride should be. One of her husband's male relatives began to tease her, which was, as the Freeds pointed out, really a breach in the traditional relationship in the family.

Daya was obviously upset, and the mother-in-law could sense it. Daya suddenly said that she felt very cold. She began to shiver, to breathe hard, and to moan. The female relatives present helped her to lie down, and covered her with quilts. She continued to moan, then became unconscious. The family knew that a ghost had come to possess Daya.

The family rallied to exorcise the ghost. One of the male members brought in some burning cow dung. Others helped Daya sit up, and they waved some of the dung smoke in her face. Daya began to jerk violently. Three of the relatives held her, and they spoke to the ghost: "Who are you," they asked. "Are you going?"

And the Freeds reported that the "ghost," speaking in Hindi through the girl, said, "Yes, I am going."

The relatives let go of Daya, who remained sitting. But suddenly she fell back. The ghost had returned. Water from a hookah (water smoking pipe) was put in her eyes and her braids were pulled. As she came to herself, she made a "high wailing sound." It meant the ghost was back again.

The relatives asked the ghost many questions, what it wanted and who it was, but Daya still seemed possessed. This time rock salt was placed between her fingers and the fingers were squeezed together. Daya wailed again.

Now there was much conversation with the ghost by the various women. They talked about noodles being denied to the ghost that morning, and how, according to the relatives, the ghost should have only cow dung, and so on.

After some time Daya fell back, seemingly unconscious again, and no further effort was made to revive her. Several hours later a *shaman* (holy man) was called in, and he revived her.

As the Freeds reported, no one present, with the possible exception of the mother-in-law, seemed to think there was anything at all unusual about the possession. The relatives were mainly interested in determining just who the ghost was, and they finally got the ghost to admit, this first time, that it was Chand Kor, one of Daya's close friends in her home village who had drowned herself in a well.

Daya continued to have possessions, and the villagers tried all the usual remedies: beating, pulling, squeezing, verbal insults, burning pig's excreta. Finally they felt that they were incapable of coping with the ghost. Several *shamans* were called in on a number of occasions. One *shaman* was successful in getting the ghost to leave Daya by agreeing that her family would make an offering of twenty-six cents, a red cloth, and a coconut to a temple near Delhi, at the time of the semiannual fair there.

The *shamans* used various remedies: They recited sacred verses, they cut some of Daya's hair and threw it into a fire, they made offerings of sweets to the ghost. They tied a blue band around her neck. The Freeds discovered most shamanistic cures stressed spells, offerings, and transferring the ghost from the one possessed to another person.

The Freeds had long talks to Daya after her possessions. She told them the symptoms of possession. Her whole body ached. She felt giddy. She slept too much. She felt very hot, and queasy in the stomach. They also discovered her emotional needs and problems. She was afraid of her new husband, in respect to sex in marriage. Her dead friend Chand Kor had had premarital sex, had gotten pregnant, and was rejected by her family (such activities were completely unacceptable to Indian social mores). Chand Kor had been encouraged to jump into the well, which she did, successfully committing suicide.

Daya was lonely in her husband's village. She was uneasy with her husband. The Freeds concluded that the spirit possession of Daya "was clearly a case of hysteria" brought on by inner tensions, a need for attention from others, and her new role as a wife.

Daya was finally cured and happy. She had been a focus for attention; she had received the sympathy she needed. Relatives came from her home village to see if she was all right; her father came and brought her some vitamins. The ghost did not come back to plague her.[5]

A decade later, in a country with highly civilized cities, a pastoral countryside, and spectacular mountains, a heinous murder was committed in an attempt to exorcise a devil. This was the case mentioned at the beginning of the book, that of Bernadette Hasler, who was so severely beaten that she died of her injuries. The whole bizarre story came out at the trial of the six persecutors, three years after the exorcism, in May 1966.

John Stocker and Magdalena Kohler were religious fanatics. Stocker had been a priest of the Pallottine Order, but had been defrocked. He, as Holy Father, and Magdalena, as Holy Mother, formed a cult that believed in the coming end of the world. They were aided in their Holy Family

Young Bernadette Hasler, victim of an exorcism by a religious cult.

by Sister Stella, a Carmelite nun, who was known as "Little Star."

Stocker and Kohler had met Sister Stella in Jerusalem in 1956. The three returned to Germany and set up a headquarters at Singen. Sister Stella supposedly had a "direct telephone to heaven," and she transmitted directions to the group, who felt they had been chosen by God to lead the survivors when the end of the world came.

Forced to leave Germany, they set up a new headquarters on the farm of Josef Hasler, Bernadette's father, in the village of Ringwil in Switzerland.

The Haslers joined the group, and turned both Bernadette and their other daughter over to this "International Family Society for the Advancement of Peace." (The children of the area called it Noah's Ark, because of all the supplies stacked up for the coming of the end of the world.)

As in a number of other religious fanatic groups of the twentieth century, the children were taken away from the influence of their parents, and were given "divine education" from the Holy Parents. Stocker and Kohler ruled the group with an iron hand, and demanded money, doled out the food to the Haslers, and even censored their mail.

They took the Haslers' car to use for "missionary trips." The adults were brainwashed. But the worst transgressions of the group were those imposed on Bernadette. They convinced her that she belonged to the devil. They said she was given over to him. They harangued her, shouted at her; they suggested that she was guilty of all kinds of improprieties.

Poor, susceptible Bernadette began to believe it even when she was accused of sexual misdeeds with the devil.

Bernadette began writing confession after confession. She became so disoriented that she believed herself guilty of anything.

How sad it was for her to write, shortly before the fatal exorcism: "I would like to have a friend of my age . . . and if I cannot have a friend, I would like at least to have a cat or a parakeet to whom I could talk." [6]

By this time Bernadette's parents would not talk to her. The other girls in Ringwil had nothing to do with her. She was quite alone, and quite susceptible to the suggestions of Kohler.

Her confessions ran to hundreds of pages. The devil visited her every day. He had black fur that glistened.

Stocker and Kohler began the exorcism rites to "drive the Devil out of" Bernadette. They enlisted the help of four other members of the cult. Twice a day they held exorcism rites during which Bernadette was beaten. The end came on the night of May 14, 1966. Bernadette was brutally beaten for four hours, with only intermittent periods of rest and prayer.

At the trial the judges and jury found the six defendants guilty of causing Bernadette serious bodily harm. The people of Zurich reacted with fury. One citizen offered to act as a hangman without pay. Another wanted to seal the offenders into a barrel of spikes and set it afire. Another suggested tying Stocker and Kohler to a telephone pole and "delivering them to the people's anger until their God deliver them." [7] Switzerland has no death penalty, so the worst these exorcists could receive was twenty years in jail. That was their sentence.

A Roman Catholic bishop noted that Stocker and Kohler had broken a number of the Church's basic tenets. There may be, he said, "non-human evil forces," but the Church does not accept them as a fact until all other possibilities have been ruled out. And then an exorcist engages in "appropriate compelling prayer" in order to effect an exorcism. Physical force is never permitted.[8]

Stocker and Kohler had indeed broken the tenets of the Church.

The devil in the twentieth century did not confine itself to bodies, but also inhabited places. Thus exorcism was prescribed to free a place from evil spirits.

One July day in 1971 a young married couple moved into a house in the Virginia suburbs with their three children. Almost immediately they heard strange noises. Footsteps were heard up and down the stairs, moving from room to room. They heard knocks on the door, but when they opened it, no one was there. Voices identical to those of their family came from various parts of the house.

The couple discussed these events and decided that they must be imagining them.

One night as they drove into the driveway after visiting some of their relatives, all the lights in the house flashed on and off.

On another evening, sometime after midnight, as the couple was watching television, they heard a crash of glass in the kitchen. They rushed into the kitchen, and saw on the floor the kitchen clock, face down, the glass broken. More startling, next to the clock was the four-inch (10-cm) spike which had held the clock to the wall, cleanly broken

THE TWENTIETH CENTURY | 81

in half. The nail hole in the wall had no mark or cracks about it.

Even more mystifying events occurred. One day as the maid was waxing the piano stool the piano suddenly shifted and lurched into the oak mantel of the fireplace, leaving a sizable dent. The maid decided that this was too much and quit her job.

At this point the young couple decided to seek help. They went to their parish priest and told him that evil spirits must be in the house.

The pastor was undecided as to what he should do. Then he thought of the Reverend John J. Nicola, the assistant director of the National Shrine of the Immaculate Conception, who had some reputation in dealing with supposedly possessed places. He called Father Nicola, and asked him to help out with this "possible infestation or obsession of a couple's home by the Devil."

The pastor and Father Nicola visited the home that very evening, and the couple recited the odd events of the past four months. Father Nicola returned to his church office and thought about the matter.

If he were to perform an official Church exorcism, he would have to consult the bishop first, and then—if he performed the formal exorcism—he would have to address the demon directly, and command him to depart from the possessed place. Father Nicola decided against this course; instead he suggested that the pastor perform an informal exorcism, giving his blessing to the house.

The pastor carried out these rites, and the strange noises and footsteps and other disturbing events stopped. Father Nicola went to see the couple about a week later, and they said all seemed well—except that there still seemed to be some noises coming from the cellar. Father Nicola went to the cellar and blessed it, which the pastor had forgotten to do.

There were no more disturbances in the house. Father Nicola, in writing to the bishop about the case, said:

> In the event of the natural causality which we have posited the blessing removed the anxiety which was responsible. [But] If perchance there was some diabolical influence, the blessing and informal exorcism was sufficient to terminate it.[9]

Father Nicola had been consulted in a number of cases in 1971, and he felt that these cases were really a reflection of the sensational popularity of occult subjects that had seized America. After the case of the possessed house received wide publicity, he said: "At the moment there is an outbreak of Satanism. There have been numerous black masses on college campuses in the past year. In fact, Satanism has not been as popular as it is today since the sixteenth and seventeenth centuries. Sparks are flying and it looks like it's going to be a full-blown thing." [10]

Father Nicola was right. Interest in the devil and in exorcism continued to grow during the next few years.

Father Nicola has never performed a formal exorcism, and he hopes he never has to, knowing of the great dangers. He is fully aware of the priests who died during the exorcism of the nuns at Loudun centuries before.

It is interesting to note that Father Nicola holds to the traditional Catholic viewpoint on the devil. According to the Roman Catholic Church the devil is a "fallen angel" who rebelled against God before the creation of the world. The devil was sentenced to hell, where he rules over the souls of evil men. But the spirits of the dead will not, according to this theory, return to earth until Judgment Day. Therefore, Father Nicola believes, spirits do not return to haunt the living now. Father Nicola does not believe that any of the cases he has handled concerned supernatural "influence." Yet, somehow by his—and the pastor's—blessings, the house of the young couple in Virginia was freed from unnatural "happenings."[11]

Although the exorcism under Father Nicola's direction was only an "informal" exorcism, the official Roman Catholic exorcism remains that of the old *Rituale Romanum*. And exorcism was reaffirmed in the revised Roman baptism rite in 1969.

The Catholic view of exorcism differs perceptibly from that of the Church of England. The *Rituale* lends the devil an existence in fact,[12] referring to the actions of the demons and how they would try to trick the exorcist. They are referred to as a "definite entity" that must be reckoned with. The Anglican Church has a different view and stated its position on exorcism in a pamphlet issued in 1972.

In 1969 the Bishop of Exeter, The Right Reverend Robert Mortimer, was so alarmed at the "unhealthy and near-hysterical" publicity in the press about exorcisms and so "disturbed" by the number of requests for help about exorcising that he was receiving, that he convened a commission to consider the place of exorcism in the life of the Church. In the foreword to the findings of the commission, the bishop spoke of the "increasing recourse to black magic and occult practices" which revealed "the presence and the power of evil forces and the contaminating influence of an evil atmosphere in particular places and environments."[13]

The bishop felt there was a need to restore the practice of exorcism to its proper place. So the findings of the commission were printed to examine publicly the place of exorcism in the Church and to offer priests practical help by giving sample prayers and forms of service.

After discussing exorcism as expressed in the New Testament the commission concluded that the current disturbances could not be dismissed as "so much hysteria." It went on to explain that exorcism was "the binding of evil powers" by the triumph of Jesus Christ. They reaffirmed that the New Testament assumes the existence of "nonhuman powers of evil."

The report details the various ways places are exorcised, noting that poltergeist activities remain a mystery, and that there can be "demonic interference."

The first step in exorcism is to determine whether a patient's illness has a physical or mental cause. ("The need for exorcism, however, when all other steps have been taken, may still arise. . . .")

An appendix to the commission's report includes prayers, the steps for exorcism and blessing of a place (". . . deliver this place from all evil spirits . . . and all deceits of the evil one; and bid them . . . depart to the place appointed them . . .") and of a person (". . . recommended that doctor and psychiatrist are aware of the steps that are being taken by the Church . . ."; "Because of the possibility of self-injury, the patient could well be seated in a deep armchair throughout the service . . ."; ". . . grant that the chains of evil binding this person may be loosed . . ."; "I command you, every evil spirit, in the Name of God . . . depart from this creature of God . . .") [14]

With the prayers and blessings, the commission hoped

to provide a "how-to" primer for the exorcists of the Church.

But not all churchmen agreed with the Bishop of Exeter.

Canon John D. Pearce-Higgens, one of England's most prominent and successful exorcists, took exception to the position of the Church of England on exorcism.

He did not believe in evil spirits, or devils, or demons that possessed; he was convinced that the possessing "entity" is merely "an earthbound, possibly confused spirit who is attached to a person or place."

The canon rejected the "demon" theory and considered the spirits "human spirits, lost souls in need of help and prayer," though he was not so presumptuous as to state flatly that "demons" or "devil forces" did not exist. He recognized "the existence of a demonic element in human nature and sometimes in its environment."

His quarrel with the Church was that it did not concern itself enough with the idea of human survival after death. To him, haunted minds and haunted houses could be caused by "misguided spirits." He felt that the "entities" died, but that it is possible to "have died without knowing you are dead."

Thus Canon Pearce-Higgens spoke kindly to a possessing spirit, rather than commandingly and imperiously to a "devil or a demon."

The canon began his work on haunted houses. He used mediums, who in their trances advised him about the particular spirit possessing the place. Later he was able to continue the work by himself. Each time he had a success, the publicity brought him more requests for help. He finally evolved a set form of service, a type of requiem mass with special prayers, which he was able to send to those priests requesting it. This requiem mass is said "for the release of the earthbound spirit." Then the canon (or priest) goes through the house with blessed water, and makes the sign of "a Celtic Cross . . . on each wall, door, window and mirror in the rooms that seem to have been affected by the spirit entity."

The canon considered the Church's formal exorcism to be more powerful but "medieval." Whenever he had to use it he changed the words so that the "spirit is commanded to be taken . . . and bound fast as with chains and cast into darkness, from which there is no return save through repentance. . . ." Such exorcism he used only "when real damage or evil is being caused," for the canon felt that when there was possession by low-grade spirits, treating them as demons and using a stronger exorcism just didn't work.

The following case was among the many Canon Pearce-Higgens performed.

An old farmhouse in the English countryside seemed to be afflicted by evil spirits, since there was much poltergeist activity. (A poltergeist is, by definition, a ghost or spirit supposed to manifest its presence by noises, including knocking.) The clerical exorcist who had been called in claimed that there was an evil demon in the attic. He performed an exorcism, but the demon remained. He went back and performed a second exorcism, which he claimed was successful. However, the noises and the knockings resumed, and the occupants called Pearce-Higgens.

The canon went to the house with a medium (one who contacts ghosts) and together they went up to the attic. According to reports of this event, the medium said that there was a dead soldier from the English civil war of the seventeenth century in the attic. He had received a head wound in the war, and had been since that time trying to escape from the attic. The medium reportedly then went into a trance, and seemed to be controlled by the entity, which seemed to be trying to fight the canon.

Suddenly Pearce-Higgens realized that the soldier was desperately trying to leave the room. He opened the door and allowed him to go. Said the canon: "I have never in my life seen anyone, whether conscious or in a trance, rush down three flights of stairs at the speed that the medium did! I chased after him for fear he should fall down and hurt himself, until he got to the front door, which I threw open for him. Once outside the medium halted, and presently returned to normal consciousness."

There were never any strange noises or knockings in the house again. The canon concluded that there was not a demon in the attic, but an unhappy human being "on the other side of life" desperately trying to escape.

The canon believed that the previous exorcism did not work on the soldier because the soldier did not think of himself as a demon, but rather a human being.[15]

Father Christopher Neil-Smith is another exorcist who is famous today in England. He, too, does not always perform official exorcisms, although the Bishop of London has licensed him to practice such rites. Many times he has used his own judgment as to whether or not to act speedily, without consulting higher authority, to help in possession cases.

One such emergency arose recently when Father Christopher Neil-Smith's telephone rang in the early hours of the morning. A very distressed woman sought the priest's help.

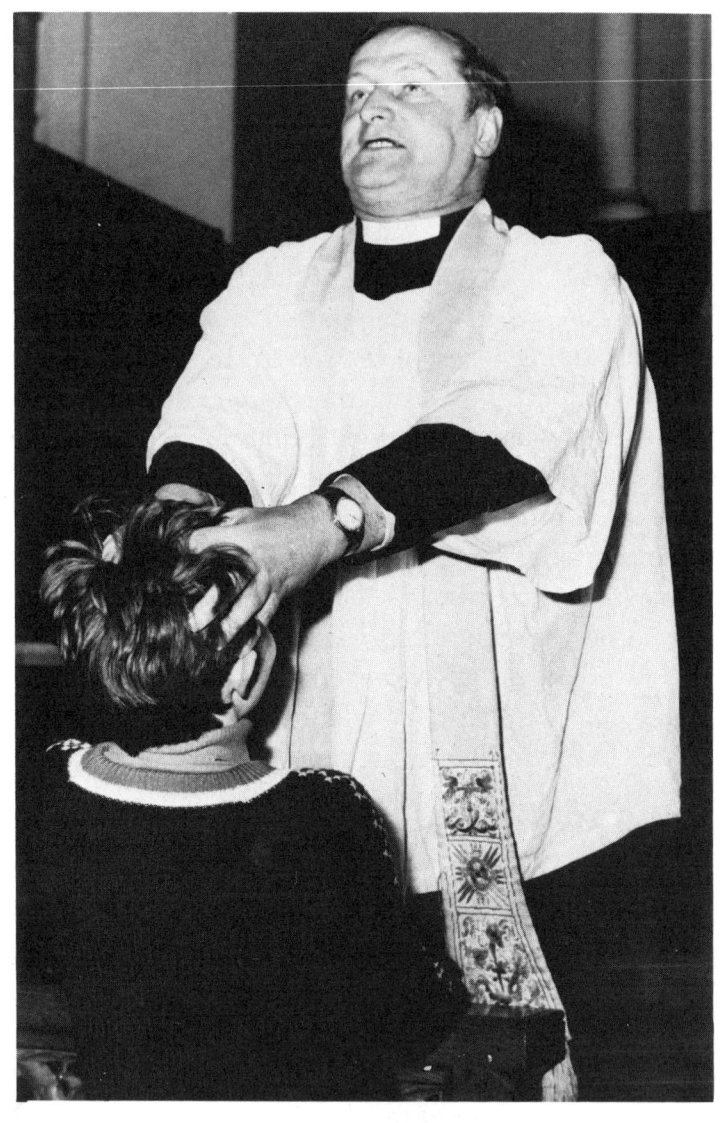

**Reverend Christopher Neil-Smith
is one of the few clerics
authorized by the Bishop of London
to conduct exorcisms.**

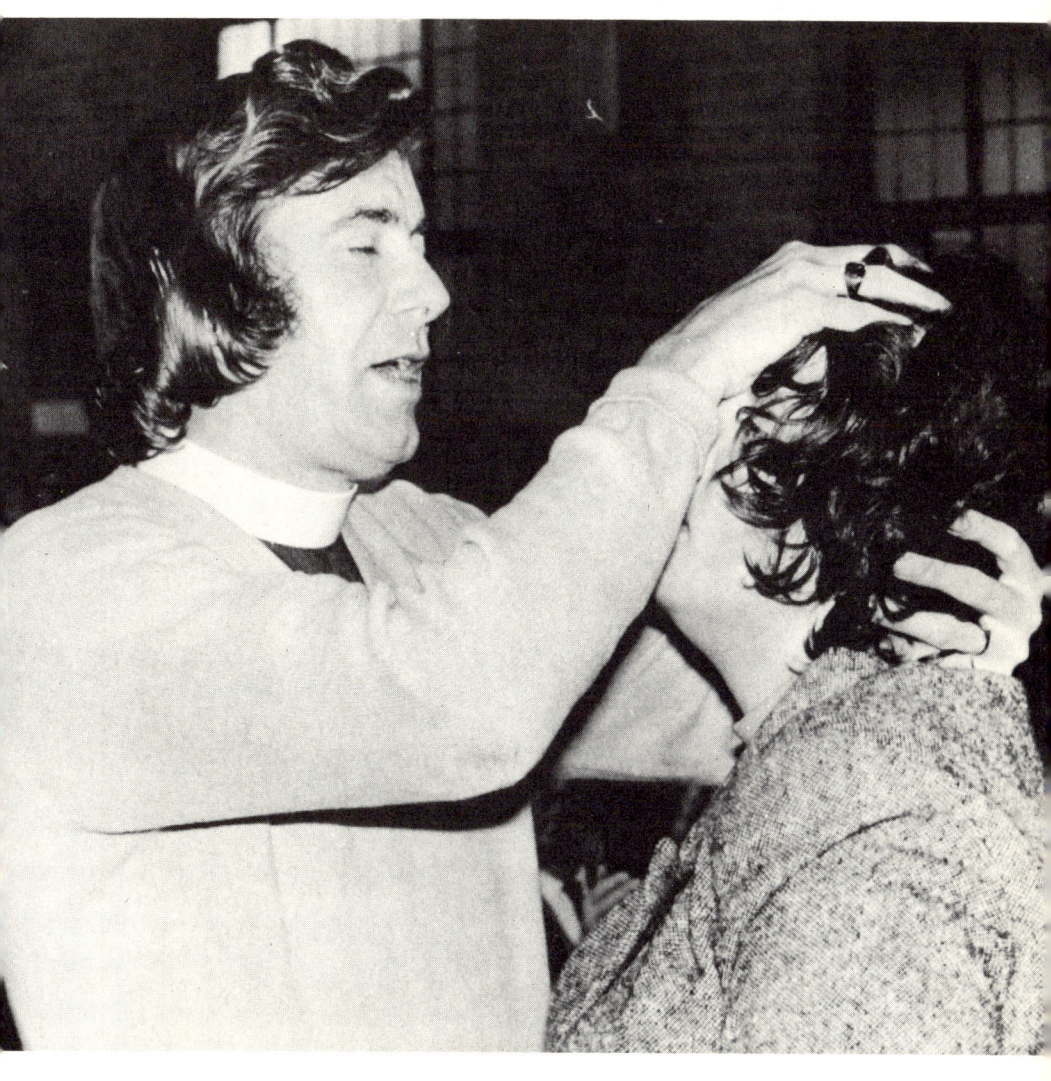

In 1975 an exorcism
was conducted at
St. Paul's Church in England.

These four people participated in an all-night exorcism. The next day, Christine Taylor (upper right) was found brutally murdered.

She said that her husband, an actor, was "going berserk." The father quickly went to the house and reported later that he immediately felt the "presence of demonic evil, and acted accordingly, making the sign of the cross and praying rapidly for the demon to depart." As soon as this informal exorcism was performed, the actor relaxed, and became calm and rational. He was never again troubled by any oppressive "evil spirits." [16]

Another case, which was revealed in 1974, concerned a sixteen-year old girl in the north countryside of England. The girl and her friends often played with a Ouija board, and it was through the medium of the board that a dead pop star talked to her. The girl became obsessed, and felt she was possessed by the ghost of her dead idol. The girl reported that the spirit made sexual suggestions to her. She became at times totally uncontrollable, screaming obscenities, and she began to think that the dead star wanted her to kill herself so "they could be together." The local priest was called in, but although he performed an exorcism, the girl still was irrational. She was taken to a psychiatric hospital, where she improved, but when she returned home, her erratic actions returned. This time the priest came and exorcised the house with Church ritual. The "evil" disappeared, and the girl became normal and rational again.[17]

In 1973 there was a mass possession in the United States, which if had happened centuries earlier would have undoubtedly necessitated an exorcism.

One spring day, in Berry, Alabama, a fifth-grade girl who had a skin rash was disturbing the class by her incessant scratching. The teacher asked her to sit outside in the hall, which she did willingly. At recess her friends came out of class and began chatting with her. Then they, too, one after the other, began scratching themselves. The students returned to their classrooms. Now children in one classroom after another were affected. By early afternoon they began complaining of burning eyes and throats, numbness, and chest pains. The principal was alarmed, and decided to evacuate the school. As a newspaper reported later, "frantic parents arrived to take their children, some of whom had scratched themselves bloody, convinced along with school and local authorities that some disease or toxic substance or perhaps a swarm of biting insects was to blame."[18] For a week over one hundred of the children scratched, fainted, vomited, cried, and screamed. More than seventy of the children were taken by ambulance to the hospital; twenty of those were unconscious.

Finally the epidemic subsided, and official investigation proved that no toxic substance was involved. The examining medical teams reported that the symptoms were due to "hyperventilation," or overbreathing—a contagion of hysteria. Psychologists noted that many of the victims were sensitive children, or were those who sought attention.[19]

It is a sign of the growing concern with mental and emotional disturbances that the parents did not seek a religious solution to the problem by calling in the clergy.

The line between an emotional or physical condition and belief in possession by the devil is indeed fine. A case occurred in the fall of 1973 in Daly City, California, which received much publicity, and also criticism from some Church members.

Some time before—in 1972—a couple with a young son were disturbed by strange occurrences in their home. Objects would fly about the house. Shoes, knives, and fireplace pokers would go through the air, breaking windows and damaging walls and ceilings. Fires would break out mysteriously. There was so much banging and crashing that the couple found it almost impossible to sleep more than a few hours each night.

One time the baby awoke crying in his crib; a rocking chair was found in the crib on top of him. These strange events went on for some time; finally the couple sought help. First they went to a team of psychic exorcists, but with no positive results. Then they went to a religious fundamentalist group which prayed over them. This was partially successful, for there were no disturbances for eight months. Then the incidents started again, even more violently: Sometimes the couple felt as though someone was trying to choke them. Sometimes they were knocked to the floor. Finally a Jesuit priest, Father Karl Patzelt, of San Francisco was asked to see if he could help the couple.

Father Patzelt went to the couple's house and did indeed feel that these bizarre occurrences were "caused by the Evil One." He did not feel that the couple was possessed, but rather that the devil must be evicted from the family's home. The priest went to his archbishop and secured permission to perform his first exorcism.

Father Patzelt performed the official Roman Catholic rite of exorcism on fourteen separate occasions. He burned incense in every room of the house and recited the prayers and chants. He said that at one point the demons mysteriously set fire to a wastebasket in the kitchen and took a bite from a sandwich on the table. The demons seemed

Father Karl Patzelt was called in
when mysterious fires and other strange
happenings plagued a young
Californian couple.

hard to defeat, but Father Patzelt continued the exorcisms. Suddenly, at the end of twenty-nine days, there was peace.

Of the exorcism, Father Patzelt said: "There is value in all of this if it brings out the reality of the devil. If the devil is real, then God must be."

But others within the church in the area were uneasy about the publicity the exorcism received. Some of the Jesuits felt it was an embarrassment that the case had been brought to public attention. Other churchmen were also distressed. "The whole thing might be blasphemous if it wasn't just plain funny," said Father Richard Byfield, an Episcopal minister at Saint Elizabeth's Church. Father Byfield felt that the disturbances were not the work of demons, but rather of ghosts. "Using the solemn rites of exorcism, against such playful spirits," he said, "is like aiming twenty-inch guns at mosquitoes." [20]

The subject of exorcism completely captured the minds of millions of people when the movie *The Exorcist* appeared all over the world in 1974. The film was based on a book by William Peter Blatty. While the book had been a best-seller, the film was even more so—it created a sensation; as *Newsweek* said, it was "The Exorcism Frenzy." [21]

Blatty had patterned his book—which he started to write in 1969—on a very real case of possession and exorcism that had occurred twenty years before when Blatty had been a student at Georgetown University in the District of Columbia.

A fourteen-year-old Protestant boy in Mount Rainier, Maryland, was "possessed by the devil." [22]

The boy was severely disturbed by poltergeist phenom-

**William Peter Blatty,
author of "The Exorcist"**

ena. His mattress slid across the floor when he was asleep; when he was in his armchair, it tilted over. Pictures and chairs moved about; strange noises were heard in the house. In despair the parents took the boy to Georgetown University Hospital. While there he shouted and cursed in Latin, and was so impossible to handle that he was strapped to his bed.

There seemed to be no physical or psychological causes for his actions, and it was suggested that the boy be taken to St. Louis for an exorcism.

The bishop was consulted and gave his permission for the exorcism. A priest was assigned to the case, and he started to prepare himself for what he knew might be an ordeal. He began a fast, eating only bread and drinking only water. He lost forty pounds. Then he was ready to begin the exorcism, using the *Rituale Romanum* formula. He prayed, he recited the psalms, and commanded the "unclean spirit" to depart. The priest sprinkled holy water and placed his hands on the boy's forehead. A crucifix was always in view.

As the exorcism was performed over the boy, he "broke into a violent tantrum of screaming, cursing and voicing of Latin phrases—a language he had never studied. . . ." [23]

The ceremony was performed twenty times over a two-month period. During the time that the boy was rational, he was converted to Catholicism. Finally, one day while the boy was thrashing about, "the possessing spirit identified himself as one of the fallen angels mentioned in the Bible and then departed." "The boy later went to a Catholic high school and then to Georgetown University and today still lives in the Washington, D.C., area." [24]

The young boy—now a man—has no recollection of his

strange experience, and according to Blatty no idea that he was ever possessed by the devil.

The priest went back to his regular clerical duties and promised his superiors not to discuss the case.

Reportedly a copy of the diary the priest kept during the period of exorcism came to Blatty's attention and provided the material for his book.

For the book and the movie Blatty changed the role of the boy to a twelve-year-old girl, Regan, daughter of an actress who is making a film on the Georgetown campus.

The plot is simple enough. The girl has violent spasms, her bed shakes, a heavy dresser moves about. Many doctors examine her. She spits in the face of one. She uses obscene words, shrieks hysterically, flails her arms, and twists from side to side, with her eyes rolled upward. No one can diagnose Regan's afflictions. She becomes more violent, her voice harsh when screaming. The doctors suggest exorcism. The resident Jesuit psychiatrist Father Karras refuses because of "faltering faith." A saintly Father Merrin attempts to exorcise the devil. He nearly succeeds, then dies suddenly of a heart attack. Father Karras then offers his help, saying at the end "take me" to the demon so that the girl might live. He plunges through a window to lie crumpled on the ground below, but can gasp a last-breath confession. He has taken the devil with him.

Regan comes out of her dreadful ordeal with no recollection of the horrifying events.[25]

Why was the book—and the movie—so sensational and successful? It *was* a shocker. Some called it pure pornography. The critics called the book "a terrifying mixture of fact and fancy;" [26] "hair-raising entertainment;" [27] "a horror story . . . taut screaming with agony . . .";[28] "demonology

Father Mark A. C. Karras

at its most horrifying, suspense that never lets up . . . a real shocker. The exorcism scene is one you won't soon forget." [29]

The public reacted to the film dramatically; some movie-goers fainted, some vomited, some began to find demons in themselves.[30] One psychiatrist said there was "no way you can sit through the film without receiving some lasting negative or disturbing effects." [31]

Members of the clergy began receiving telephone calls asking for exorcisms.

Members of the clergy themselves had various reactions. Some were concerned with the obscene language coming from a child's mouth, but in reality from the demon possessing the child. Some said the film showed "good triumphing over evil. Evil comes from another source, the devil." [32] Others worried that the picture would encourage a new wave of exorcisms. A twelve-year-old Washington girl began having symptoms like the girl in the movie. After much questioning she finally admitted she had read the book.[33]

Father Edmund G. Ryan, S.J., of Georgetown University, said at the time of the filming that as "new causes and cures have been discovered, the instances of actual possession have lessened." [34]

Father Ryan has been a student of exorcism and openly discusses it. He says that exorcism is "the act of driving out or warding off demons or evil spirits from persons, places, or things that are believed to be possessed or infested by them, or are liable to become victims or instruments of their malice. . . . Exorcism really is nothing more than a prayer to God, is sometimes made publicly, but always in the name of the Church, and in the name of Christ, to restrain the power of the demons over men and things.

"... What the Church would hold," Father Ryan says, "is that all demons are subject to God and the Catholic Church does not perform exorcisms in its own name but in the name of Christ...." Father Ryan has never performed an exorcism, but he believes that the "moral life of a priest must be beyond reproach and I don't consider myself in that line of holiness." [35]

That view is not shared by some other clergymen. One such is the Catholic exorcist Monsignor Luigi Nevarese, who is the official exorcist for the Pope. He has performed the Church ritual over sixty times. He claims that the demons have never affected him, but admits that they cause great facial changes in the victims. In one case, he said, the possessed man's skin "turned white as paper, his teeth became transparent, his eyes bulged with balls of flame and fire issued from his mouth." [36]

And so exorcism continues today, although the Church rites are fewer than in previous centuries. Most of the modern exorcisms are conducted quietly and receive little publicity. However, there are bizarre cases when religious zeal has replaced good sense.

Toward the end of 1976 in Yakima, Washington, a three-year-old boy was found dead, wrapped in a sheet, on a cot in a sealed bedroom of a house where a religious cult lived. Five members, including the boy's mother, were found guilty of beating the boy to death. They had beaten him every day for four months to get rid of the devil they thought was possessing him. Edward Leon Cunningham was the self-proclaimed cult pastor and "prophet of God." During a pretrial hearing, Cunningham answered the questions put to him by the prosecutor with biblical quotations.

Why did they beat the child?

"Do not withhold discipline from a child; if you beat him with a rod he will not die." (Proverbs 13:23.)

What good would that do?

"And Jesus rebuked the devil and he departed out of him." (Matthew 17:18.)

But the child had died. What did that show?

"Thou shall not suffer a witch to live." (Exodus 22:18.)

The beatings, said the cult, were the only way to deal with the devil. This was their form of exorcism. What was important was the devil, not the child.[37]

An exorcism case that caused much concern and received wide publicity occurred in the Würzburg diocese in West Germany in 1976. It was the first exorcism in that diocese in two centuries.

Josef Stangl, Bishop of Würzburg, authorized the exorcism of a student teacher, Anneliese Michel of Klingenberg-on-Main. Anneliese was an epileptic who suffered chronic fits. She had had no medical attention for a year when the exorcists took over. Two Roman Catholic priests tried to exorcise five devils from her body. But she wasted away—to seventy pounds at the end. Finally she died, and when the civil authorities entered the case they said the cause of her death was starvation.

A dozen manslaughter suits were filed against the clergy involved in the exorcism, including one against the bishop who authorized it. The death was considered a tragedy. In Germany critics called exorcism a "medieval rite which should not be practiced in contemporary times."

Anneliese's parents disagree with this view. Her mother

said: "I am shocked that despite the fact that my daughter has obviously been killed by the devil, no one believes in him." [38]

Katherine Elizabeth Council was a twenty-one-year-old student in a Brooklyn school. She had suffered from seizures for several years. For a time her family had her in a psychiatric hospital, but she had been discharged. When she continued to have fits her mother and three friends drove her south to see a noted "faith healer" in Monks Corner, South Carolina. They sought advice on how to rid the young woman of the "demons" who were causing her epileptic-type seizures. The faith healer told the mother the fits were definitely caused by "demons." If she would put a scarf saturated with turpentine and ammonia around the face and neck of her daughter the "demons" would be driven out. The healer also prescribed a dark brown potion to be placed on the girl's forehead. He warned the mother that Katherine must never look at a full moon.

Full of this advice, mother and daughter and their friends got into their car and drove north toward their home in Brooklyn. On the New Jersey Turnpike, near Mount Holly, New Jersey, the daughter suffered a seizure and tried to jump out of the car. The mother and another tied her hands and feet together to keep her from kicking the driver, and they put the prescribed scarf over her face and neck. Then the driver stopped at a turnpike service station to ask for medical help. Katherine was taken to Burlington County Memorial Hospital—where she was pronounced dead on arrival. An autopsy showed the cause of death to be asphyxiation.

The mother was brought to trial and accused of murdering her daughter.

"Hallelujah! Thank you Jesus!" she cried.[39]

One day recently about one hundred young people, many of them self-styled "hippies," attended a "healing festival" in a lovely meadow behind a farmhouse near Watsonville, Oregon. They were there to gain spiritual help from one another.

Suddenly a young girl fell to the ground. She jiggled her legs up and down, writhed and thrashed about, kicked her legs, arched her back, and whirled her head about. She moaned and cried out.

Clutching at her throat, she screamed, "There are little men in my throat." She repeated over and over, "There are little men in my throat."

Those about her were stunned, and tried to comfort her. One young witness was so overcome that she fell to her knees, crying and praying, "Oh, God, help her! Help her!"

The seizure lasted about two hours, with the girl moaning, crying, writhing, her face contorted, speaking fragments of Latin. It was a chilling, frightening scene to the young spiritualists who had come for group comfort and exchanges. Suddenly the afflicted girl was silent. She opened her eyes, and the first words she spoke were, "What happened?"

Those around her told her what they had witnessed and heard. The girl knew nothing of the experience. She emitted a soft "Wow!," and that was the end of the incident.

Was she possessed of the devil? Did she need an exorcism? Was she ill, mentally or physically? Was she posing? Was she aping Regan of *The Exorcist?*

The young spiritualists who have long since scattered will really never know.[40]

Fortunately most modern exorcisms are not carried out by misguided self-styled exorcists. The Reverend Bill Smith, of the Waialae Baptist Church in Honolulu, Hawaii, quietly conducted exorcisms for three years. The pastor was reluctant to discuss his exorcisms because of what he called an inordinate interest in the occult, fanned by the spate of movies and books on exorcism. He felt that some people "cashed in" on exorcism.

That was true, until his "battles with the devil" were reported in the Honolulu newspapers as a result of an unexpected exorcism in public.

A pharmaceutical society was meeting in Honolulu, and Dr. François Saculla, a psychiatrist, had asked the pastor to attend in order to discuss the religious aspects of an exorcism.

Saculla had brought a patient, a girl with a case of multiple personalities, to the meeting to show his techniques of hypnosis. As soon as Reverend Smith saw her he realized that emanating from the girl was a "Satanic force" that he had met with before in other exorcisms. Smith gave a command "in the name of Jesus Christ of Nazareth" to the demonic force and the girl went into a seizure. The audience at the meeting gasped. Then the seizure ended, and the girl "regained a calm composure." The demonic force was gone, but the pastor was concerned about the public attention this exorcism was sure to receive.

He has, he says, "spiritually discerning abilities" that God has given to him, and thus he knows when he is dealing with the devil. This sensibility, plus a study of books

Reverend Bill Smith
of Honolulu, Hawaii

on exorcism and of the Scriptures enables him to perform exorcisms. The people he has helped are varied: "Some are losing their minds or on the brink of emotional breakdowns. Others are physically sick. And some know exactly what is wrong with them." The pastor first began with counseling and ferreting out the problem bothering the "possessed" individual.

Smith says the demons he battles are real, not just in the imagination. He calls the devil an "intelligent being who knows what he is doing. Unlike God, Satan is not omnipotent. He can't be at all places at the same time. He has to have demons serve him."

It is obvious to Pastor Smith when a demonic force is present in the exorcisms, because of "the other-worldly nature of the force that has taken over the patient's mind and body."

Sometimes, he says, his contact with the demon is "an audible one. It is really weird. You can hear sometimes a man's voice in a woman."

Sometimes the devil tried to trick him by "acting nicely," but then it turns mean and vile. The person begins groaning, and feels cold to the touch.

Pastor Smith works with an assistant, for once he was thrown thirty feet across the room by a seventy-pound woman. "I was absolutely whipped after some sessions," he commented, "because these people have supernatural strength."

So he uses an assistant at every exorcism. In case the devil caused the patient to become violent, the assistant, by uttering a commandment in the name of Jesus, can control the devil.

This modern exorcist says exorcism "validates the Scrip-

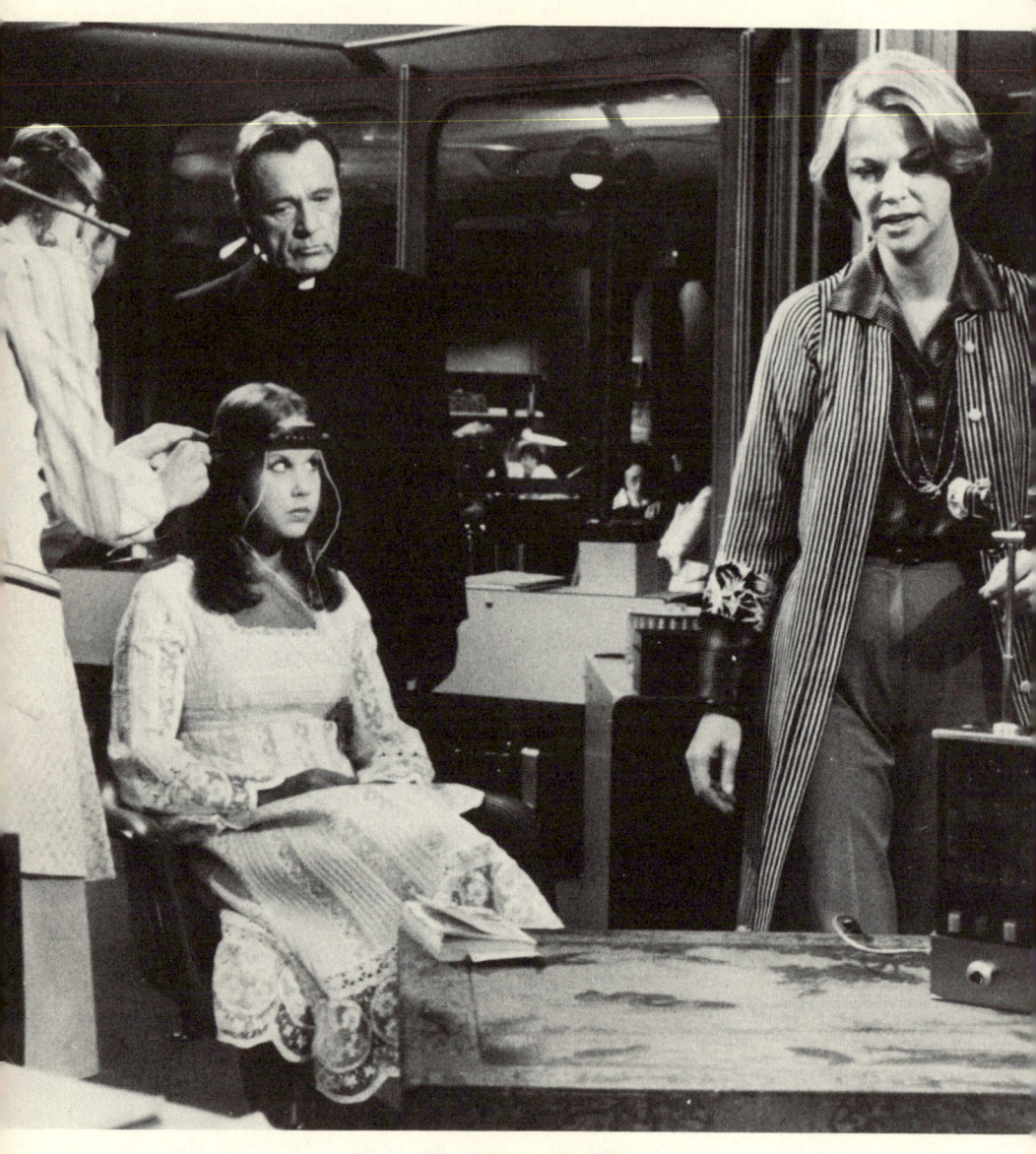

A scene from the sequel to "The Exorcist"— "Exorcist II: The Heretic"

tures. The truths presented in the Bible are real. God is powerful and Satan is real. Satan is a person who can deceive, trick and kill you. . . . The Scriptures show me how Jesus dealt with the problem and how demons recognized him and responded." [41]

So in the last quarter of the twentieth century demons continue to afflict society and exorcists continue to do battle with them for human souls.

NOTES

Introduction

1. Roger Baker, *Binding the Devil; Exorcism Past and Present* (New York, Hawthorn Books, 1974).
2. Dom Robert Petitpierre, ed., *Exorcism; The Findings of a Commission Convened by the Bishop of Exeter* (London, S.P.C.K. Holy Trinity Church, 1972).
3. *Newsweek* (January 1, 1973).
4. Baker, *Binding the Devil.*
5. *The Wall Street Journal* (October 25, 1976).
6. *Newsweek* (February 11, 1974).
7. *The Wall Street Journal* (October 25, 1976).

The Ancients

1. *Time* (February 7, 1969); *Newsweek* (February 10, 1969).
2. *Ibid.*
3. Baker, *Binding the Devil.*
4. Martin Ebon, *The Devil's Bride; Exorcism, Past and Present* (New York, Harper & Row, 1974).
5. Traugott K. Oesterreich, *Possession and Exorcism* (New York, Causeway Books, 1974).
6. *Ibid.* and Montague Summers, *The History of Witchcraft and Demonology* (London, Routledge & Kegan Paul Ltd., 1926).

7. *Ibid.*
8. Baker, *Binding the Devil.*
9. Mildred Boyd, *Man, Myth and Magic* (New York, Criterion Books, 1969).
10. Julius Jolly, *"Grundriss der indo-arischen Theologie und Altertumskunde,"* Vol. IV, No. 10, Strasburg, 1901, as quoted by Oesterreich in *Possession and Exorcism.*
11. *The Lalita-Vistara* or *Memoirs of the Early Life of S'a'kya Sinha.* Translated from the original Sanskrit, 1881, as quoted by Oesterreich in *Possession and Exorcism.*
12. A. Deissmann in *Licht vom Osten,* as quoted by Oesterreich in *Possession and Exorcism.*
13. Olga Hoyt, *Demons, Devils and Djinn* (New York, Abelard-Schuman, 1974); Ebon, *The Devil's Bride.*
14. Flavius Josephus in *Antiquities of the Jews,* as quoted by Oesterreich, in *Possession and Exorcism.*

Christ, Early Christians, and the Middle Ages

1. Mark, 1:33–39.
2. *Ibid.*
3. *Ibid.*
4. Harnack in *Die Mission,* as quoted by Traugott K. Oesterreich, in *Possession and Exorcism.*
5. Oesterreich, *Possession and Exorcism.*
6. *Ibid.*
7. *Ibid.*
8. *Ibid.*
9. *Ibid.*
10. Baker, *Binding the Devil.*
11. *Ibid.*

Fifteenth and Sixteenth Centuries

1. Oesterreich, *Possession and Exorcism.*
2. Baker, *Binding the Devil.*
3. *Ibid.*

4. Oesterreich, *Possession and Exorcism.*
5. Summers, *The History of Witchcraft and Demonology.*
6. Ebon, *The Devil's Bride.*
7. Summers, *History of Witchcraft and Demonology.*
8. *Ibid.*
9. *Ibid.*

Seventeenth and Eighteenth Centuries

1. Summers, *The History of Witchcraft and Demonology.*
2. Ebon, *The Devil's Bride.*
3. Oesterreich, *Possession and Exorcism;* F. X. Maquart, "Exorcism," in *Soundings in Satanism,* F. J. Sheed, ed.
4. Maquart, "Exorcism."
5. Summers. *History of Witchcraft and Demonology.*
6. Oesterreich, *Possession and Exorcism.*
7. *Ibid.*
8. Eric Maple, *The Dark World of Witches* (Indianapolis, Indiana, Pegasus/Bobbs-Merrill, 1970).
9. Montague Summers, *The Geography of Witchcraft* (New Hyde Park, New York, University Books, 1958); Aldous Huxley, *The Devils of Loudun* (New York, Harper & Row, 1952).
10. Summers, *The Geography of Witchcraft.*
11. Ebon, *The Devil's Bride.*
12. *Ibid.*
13. Huxley, *The Devils of Loudun.*
14. Ebon, *The Devil's Bride.*
15. Douglas Hill and Pat Williams, *The Supernatural* (New York, Hawthorn Books, 1965).
16. Oesterreich, *Possession and Exorcism.*

The Nineteenth Century

1. Summers, *The History of Witchcraft and Demonology.*
2. Oesterreich, *Possession and Exorcism.*
3. *Ibid.*
4. *Ibid.*

5. *Ibid.*
6. *Ibid.*; John L. Nevius, *Demon Possession and Allied Themes;* Ebon, *The Devil's Bride.*
7. Oesterreich, *Possession and Exorcism.*
8. Summers, *History of Witchcraft and Demonology.*
9. Maple, *The Dark World of Witches.*
10. Ebon, *The Devil's Bride;* Summers, *History of Witchcraft and Demonology.*
11. *Ibid.*
12. *Ibid.*
13. P. Kahle, "Zar Beschworungen in Aegypten," in the *Der Islam,* Vol. 11 (1912), as quoted by Oesterreich in *Possession and Exorcism.*
14. Snounck Hurgronje, "*Mekka,*" Vol. 11 (1889), as quoted by Oesterreich in *Possession and Exorcism.*
15. *Ibid.*
16. B. Klunzinger, *Bilder aus Aberägypten, der Wüste und dem roten Meere,* 1877, as quoted by Oesterreich in *Possession and Exorcism.*
17. J. Borelli, *Ethiopie Meridionale,* 1890, as quoted by Oesterreich in *Possession and Exorcism.*

The Twentieth Century

1. Vivian Gornick, *In Search for Ali Mahmoud,* as quoted by Ebon in *The Devil's Bride.*
2. Simon D. Messing, "Group Therapy and Social Status in The Zar Cult of Ethiopia," in John Middleton, ed., *Magic, Witchcraft And Curing* (American Museum [of Natural History] Sourcebooks in Anthropology. Garden City, New York, The Natural History Press, 1967); Ebon, *The Devil's Bride.*
3. *Ibid.*
4. Ebon, *The Devil's Bride.*
5. Stanley A. and Ruth S. Freed, "Spirit Possession as Illness in a North Indian Village," in Middleton, ed., *Magic, Witchcraft and Curing.*
6. *Time* (February 7, 1969); *Newsweek* (February 10, 1969).
7. *Ibid.*
8. *Ibid.*

9. *Washington Post* (November 14, 1971).
10. *Ibid.*
11. *Ibid.*
12. Baker, *Binding the Devil.*
13. Petitpierre, ed., *Exorcism; The Findings of a Commission Convened by the Bishop of Exeter.*
14. *Ibid.*
15. Ebon, *The Devil's Bride.*
16. Baker, *Binding the Devil.*
17. *Ibid.*
18. *The Wall Street Journal* (November 16, 1973), as reported in Ebon, *The Devil's Bride.*
19. *Ibid.*
20. *Newsweek* (February 11, 1974) and *Time* (January 28, 1974).
21. *Newsweek* (February 11, 1974).
22. *Washington Post* (November 6, 1972).
23. *Ibid.*
24. *Newsweek* (February 11, 1974).
25. William Peter Blatty, *The Exorcist* (New York, Harper & Row, 1971).
26. *The New York Times Book Review,* as quoted in Blatty, *The Exorcist.*
27. *Life,* as quoted in Blatty, *The Exorcist.*
28. *Boston Globe,* as quoted in Blatty, *The Exorcist.*
29. *Publishers Weekly,* as quoted in Blatty, *The Exorcist.*
30. *Newsweek* (February 11, 1974).
31. *Ibid.*
32. *Ibid.*
33. *Washington Post* (November 6, 1972).
34. *Ibid.*
35. *Ibid.*
36. *Newsweek* (February 11, 1974).
37. Honolulu *Advertiser* (November 19, 1976); Honolulu *Star-Bulletin* (November 19, 1976).
38. *Parade* (December 26, 1976).
39. *The New York Times* (January 11, 1977).
40. Witness to author.
41. David Tong interview, Honolulu *Advertiser* (December 4, 1976).

BIBLIOGRAPHY

Baker, Roger, *Binding the Devil; Exorcism Past and Present*. New York, Hawthorn Books, 1974.

Blatty, William Peter, *The Exorcist*. New York, Harper & Row, 1971.

Boyd, Mildred, *Man, Myth and Magic*. New York, Criterion Books, 1969.

Cohen, Daniel, *Voodoo, Devils and the New Invisible World*. New York, Dodd Mead & Co., 1972.

Ebon, Martin, *The Devil's Bride; Exorcism, Past and Present*. New York, Harper & Row, 1974.

Freed, Stanley A. and Ruth S., "Spirit Possession as Illness in a North Indian Village," in John Middleton, ed., *Magic, Witchcraft and Curing*. American Museum (of Natural History) Sourcebooks in Anthropology. Garden City, New York, The Natural History Press, 1967.

Hill, Douglas, and Williams, Pat, *The Supernatural*. New York, Hawthorn Books, 1965.

Hoyt, Olga, *Demons, Devils and Djinn*. New York, Abelard-Schuman, 1974.

Huxley, Aldous, *The Devils of Loudun*. New York, Harper & Row, 1952.

Maple, Eric, *The Dark World of Witches*. Indianapolis, Indiana, Pegasus/Bobbs-Merrill, 1970.

Maquart, F. X., "Exorcism," in F. J. Sheed, ed., *Soundings in Satanism*. New York, Sheed & Ward, 1972.

Messing, Simon D., "Group Therapy and Social Status in the Zar Cult of Ethiopia," in John Middleton, ed., *Magic, Witchcraft and Curing*. American Museum (of Natural History) Sourcebooks in Anthropology. Garden City, New York, The Natural History Press, 1967.
Middleton, John, ed., *Magic, Witchcraft and Curing*. American Museum (of Natural History) Sourcebooks in Anthropology. Garden City, New York, The Natural History Press, 1967.
Nevius, John L., *Demon Possession and Allied Themes*. 1894.
Oesterreich, Traugott K., *Possession and Exorcism*. New York, Causeway Books, 1974.
Petitpierre, Dom Robert, ed., *Exorcism; The Findings of a Commission Convened by the Bishop of Exeter*. London, S.P.C.K. Holy Trinity Church, 1972.
Shah, Idries, *Oriental Magic*. New York, Dutton, 1973.
Sheed, F. J., ed., *Soundings in Satanism*. New York, Sheed & Ward, 1972.
Summers, Montague, *Geography of Witchcraft*. New Hyde Park, New York, University Books, 1958.
———, *The History of Witchcraft and Demonology*. London, Routledge & Kegan Paul Ltd., 1926.

Newspapers and Magazines

Honolulu *Advertiser*, November 19, 1976, December 4, 1976.
Newsweek Magazine, February 10, 1969, January 1, 1973, February 11, 1974.
The New York Times, January 11, 1977.
Parade Magazine, December 26, 1976.
Honolulu *Star-Bulletin*, November 19, 1976.
Time Magazine, February 7, 1969, January 28, 1974.
The Wall Street Journal, November 16, 1973, October 25, 1976.
Washington Post, November 14, 1971, November 6, 1972.

INDEX

Africa, 24
Alsace, 59–62
Alternative churches, 3
Animals, possession by, 48–49, 51–53
Assyria, 6
Astrology, 3
Austria, 25, 39–41

Babylonia, 6, 8
Baptism, 24, 46–47
Barré, Pierre, 38
Begone Satan (Vogl), 59, 70
Belgium, 23
Benedict, Saint, 18–19
Bernard of Clairvaux, Saint, 19, 21–22
Bint-Reschid, 10
Blatty, William Peter, 95, 98
Braun, Leopold, 40
Brey, Charles, 62
Burner, Joseph, 59–62
Burner, Theobald, 59–62
Busch, Joseph F., 70
Byfield, Richard, 95

China, 52–54
Christians, early, 17–19
Church of England, 83–86
Council, Katherine Elizabeth, 103–104
Cunningham, Edward Leon, 101–102

Dancing mania, 23
Darling, Thomas, 29
Darrel, John, 28–32
Delirium, 63–68
Demonic possession. *See* Exorcism
Devils of Loudun, 37–39
Dual personality, 34

Ea (god), 6, 8
Ecklund, Anna, 69–73
Ecstasy, 63–68
Egypt, 9–11, 63, 67–68
Eleazar, 14–15
England, 26–32, 36–37, 45–47, 57–58, 83–87, 91
Epilepsy, 28, 34
Eridu, 6

Ernaldus, 21
Ethiopia, 65, 68
Exorcism
  in Africa, 24
  in Alsace, 59–62
  in ancient times, 6–15
  in Austria, 25, 39–41
  in Babylonia and Assyria, 6, 8
  in Belgium, 23
  in China, 52–54
  Christ and, 16–17
  early Christians and, 17–19
  in Egypt, 63–68
  in England, 26–32, 36–37, 45–47, 57–58, 83–87, 91
  in Ethiopia, 65, 68
  in fifteenth and sixteenth centuries, 24–32
  in France, 19, 21–22, 37–39, 54–57
  in Germany, 23, 42–44, 102–103
  in Hawaii, 105
  in Holland, 23, 25
  in India, 12, 14, 73–76
  in Israel, 14–17
  in Italy, 18, 19
  in Japan, 25–26, 48–49, 51
  in Malay Peninsula, 51–52
  mass possession, 23, 25, 91–92
  in Middle Ages, 19–23
  in nineteenth century, 45–66
  ordination of exorcists, 33–34
  persecution of exorcists, 26–27
  in Persia, 11–12
  Rituale Romanum, 33–36, 42, 83, 97
  in Russia, 47–48
  in seventeenth and eighteenth centuries, 33–44
  in Switzerland, 5, 76, 78–80
  in twentieth century, 67–109
Exorcist, The (movie), 4, 95, 98, 100

Fake misdiagnosed possession, 28–32, 36–37
France, 19, 21–22, 37–39, 54–57
Freed, Ruth, 73–76
Freed, Stanley, 73–76
Freud, Sigmund, 39, 41

Gadarene demon, 16–17
Germany, 23, 42–44, 102–103
Gornick, Vivian, 67
Grandier, Urbain, 37–38
Gregory the Great, 18
Gregory of Tours, 19

Haizmann, Johann Christoph, 39–41
Harnack, 17
Hartley, Edmund, 29–30
Hasler, Bernadette, 5, 76, 78–79
Hasler, Josef, 78
Hawaii, 105
Holland, 23, 25
Horoscopes, 3
Horus (god), 11
Huxley, Aldous, 37–39
Hyperventilation, 92
Hysteria, 34, 69

I Ching, 3
India, 12, 14, 73–76
Israel, 14–17
Italy, 18, 19

Japan, 25–26, 48–49, 51
Jeanne des Anges, Sister, 38, 39
Jesuits, 25, 42, 93, 95
Jesus Christ, 16–17
Jewish exorcism, 14–15
Johann of Kronstadt, 47
Josephus, Flavius, 14, 15

Kapsner, Celestine, 70
Khonsu (god), 9, 10

Kohler, Magdalena, 76, 78–80

Lactance, Father, 39
Leo Africanus, 24
Levitation, 34–35, 59
Luke, Saint, 16

Malay Peninsula, 51–52
Manuale Exorcismorum, 36
Marduk (god), 6, 8
Mark, Saint, 16
Mass possession, 23, 25, 91–92
Matthew, Saint, 16
Maya, 14
Mecca, 63
Mediums, 86–87
Meitinger, Sebastian, 40
Michel, Anneliese, 102–103
Middle Ages, 19–23
More, George, 30, 31
Mortimer, Robert, 83–85
Moslem religion, 24
Movies, 4, 95, 98, 100
Murrell, James, 57–58

National Synod of Rheims, 27
Neferou Ra, Queen of Egypt, 9–10
Neil-Smith, Christopher, 87, 91
Nevarese, Luigi, 101
Nevius, John L., 53
Nichiren sect, 49
Nicola, John J., 81–83
Norbert of Magdeburg, Saint, 22

Ouija boards, 3

Patzelt, Karl, 93, 95
Paul VI, Pope, 3
Peach, Edward, 46–47
Pearce-Higgens, John D., 85–87
Persia, 11–12
Pius IX, Pope, 56
Poirier, Hélène-Joséphine, 54–57

Poltergeists, 84, 86, 93, 95, 97
Protestant Church, 26–27, 45

Rameses II, King of Egypt, 9, 10
Requiem mass, 85–86
Riesinger, Theophilus, 69–72
Rituale Romanum, 33–36, 42, 83, 97
Roman Catholic Church, 26–27, 33–36, 45–48, 82–83, 93, 95
Roper, Margaret, 28
Russia, 47–48
Ryan, Edmund G., 100–101

Saculla, François, 105
Saint Vitus dance, 23
Satanic cults, 3, 56
Satanism. *See* Exorcism
Schrantzer, Abbé, 61
Shamash (god), 8
Smith, Bill, 105, 107, 109
Solomon, King of Israel, 14, 15
Somers, William, 30–31
Spanish Inquisition, 42
Stangl, Josef, 102
Starchie family, 29–30
Steiger, Joseph, 70, 71
Stella, Sister, 78
Stocker, John, 76, 78–80
Surin, Jean-Pierre, 39
Switzerland, 5, 76, 78–80

Tehutiem-heb, 10
Tranquille, Father, 39

United States, 69–72, 80–83, 91–93, 95, 101–104
Ursuline Convent, Loudun, France, 37–39

Vogl, Carl, 70

Weston, William, 26–27
Witchcraft, 3, 25, 28, 29, 58
Wright, Katherine, 28

Zar cults, 63–68
Zoroaster, 11–12
Zoroastrianism, 11

ABOUT THE AUTHOR

Olga Hoyt, presently a happy resident of Honolulu, Hawaii, with her husband, Edwin, is the author of five books for young people.

An avid researcher and reteller of tales, Ms. Hoyt conducted original interviews for some of the accounts detailed in this book.